Also by Elizabeth Berg
Available from Random House Large Print

The Confession Club
Night of Miracles
The Story of Arthur Truluv

I'll Be Seeing You

I'll Be Seeing You

A MEMOIR

Elizabeth Berg

R A N D O M   H O U S E
LARGE PRINT

Cover design: Victoria Allen
Cover photograph of Jeanne and Art Hoff,
courtesy of the author

The Library of Congress has established
a Cataloging-in-Publication record
for this title.

ISBN: 978-0-593-29515-1

www.penguinrandomhouse.com/
large-print-format-books

FIRST LARGE PRINT EDITION

Printed in the United States of America

10 9 8 7 6 5 4 3 2 1

This Large Print edition published in accord
with the standards of the N.A.V.H.

To my sister, Vicki Hansen,
with admiration for her
clear-eyed compassion, and
with much love

Or it might be, she thought, having lived long enough, she'd come to think of everyone close to her with a helpless tenderness, accepting that life was hard and people did their best.

—STEWART O'NAN,
Emily, Alone

Prologue

I am seventy years old. I am astonished to be writing this, as doubtful of the truth of it as if I had just written, "I am a peacock." I remind myself of the two old ladies (as I thought of them then) I saw in the grocery store one day, their carts angled companionably next to each other. They were enjoying a nice chat, and as I passed them, I heard one say to the other, "I still feel like a **girl** inside."

As do I. I still feel like a girl inside, someone with grass stains on her knees and a roller-skate key around her neck. Someone who catches minnows in a jar and practices kissing on a pillow and finds joy in the smallest of things: the weight of a parakeet sitting

on my finger; the smell of sun on grass; don-
ning new shoes for the first day of school.

The outside me is another story. I have
gotten to the most-days-are-good-some-
days-are-bad portion of my own show. I
am used to having various aches and pains.
I am used to not having flexibility or good
balance. I am used to losing a word or a
name, then eventually finding it—or not.
Losing objects, then finding them. Or not. I
am not at the point where I find my hair-
brush in the refrigerator, but I suppose it's
possible that that, too, is coming.

It's been gradual, these changes I've experienced, and so it has been merciful. I have
adjusted to them pretty well, I think, and in
fact oftentimes I find symptoms of aging less
painful than funny. Just last night, a friend
told me about an eighty-something friend of
hers saying he was great except he couldn't
get up off the toilet seat. We found that hys-
terical. He did, too.

Mostly, I feel grateful to be the age that
I am now. You lose some things, growing
older, but you gain other, more important
things: tolerance, gratitude, perspective, the
unexpected pleasure in doing things more

slowly. It's not a bad trade, except that you are increasingly aware that your number will be up sooner rather than later. I know that it's probably time for me to see a lawyer, to have The Talk with my daughters about how I want my worldly goods divided, how I want a pod burial in which my ashes will nourish a tree. I'm putting that talk off, though. **I still feel like a girl inside.**

I think as long as a parent is alive, it's easier to feel young. It's easy to feel that in some respects you are still being taken care of, even when it becomes more you who takes care of them. But parents don't stay alive forever, and the period before they die can be uniquely difficult. What helped me most in dealing with my own parents' fading was to hear what others were going through. And so:

This book is a diary of my parents' decline. When I experienced them losing power and independence, as well as the home they were loath to leave (to the extent that I did; since I was the faraway daughter, my sister did nearly all the heavy lifting), I learned a lot about them, and just as much about myself.

I learned that the frustration and anger that come up in these situations go both ways: you're frustrated and/or angry with your parents and they're frustrated and/or angry with you. I saw how deep the despair can be in realizing that you can no longer properly care for yourself, but I also saw how accepting the love and help that are offered can foster a whole new level of appreciation and understanding between parents and children. I learned that in the middle of what can feel like a gigantic, painful mess, there can suddenly be the saving grace of humor or the salve of a certain kind of insight.

I also learned that I am at the in-between place, having cared for my parents and now soon to need help from my own children, no doubt. I'm not yet **old**, but I'm certainly getting there, and I am more aware every day of what can befall me, my partner, and my friends, all of whom, I think, still feel inside like the girls or boys they used to be. So when I consider the story of my parents' failing, I am picking up stones on the path to put into my pocket. I hope what I learned from them will help me and my children.

But I have to say that the biggest thing I learned in caring for my parents is that their life together, despite its hardships and frustrations, was a love story—deeply, wholly, and completely. It was the kind of love story you hardly ever see or hear about anymore. I was privileged to bear witness to it. I am bearing witness to it still.

I'll Be Seeing You

The failing of an aging parent is one of those old stories that feels abrasively new to the person experiencing it. At eighty-nine years of age, my father has begun, in his own words, to "lose it." This is a man who was for so many years terrifying to me. He was tall and fit, a lifer in the U.S. Army whose way of awakening me in the morning when I was in high school was to stand at the threshold of my bedroom and say, "Move out." He was never quick to smile, he put the fear of God into every young man I dated in high school, and if he said to do something, you did it immediately, no excuses. He yelled at us a lot, and, like many men of his generation, he believed in corporeal punishment.

Over the years he mellowed, though he was still quick to rise to anger, if the occasion seemed to call for it. But he mellowed, and none of us who really knew him could help it: not only did we love him, we liked him. The most striking thing about him was his truthfulness: the man would never lie. And he was a big softie when it came to animals and to my mother: she was the place where he put his tenderness. He had a dry sense of humor, and he was vastly intelligent.

But now. My mother says he sits sometimes with his hands over his face, unmoving, and she thinks he is depressed. Also, she has noticed things happening more and more often: a repetition of questions that she has already answered many times over. A kind of paranoia: he claims things have been taken from the glove compartment of the car he no longer drives. My mother finds him in the closet of the TV room and he says he is looking for someone who came out of there to mess with things on his TV tray. When the lid of the garbage can goes missing (after a day of high winds), he says it must be hooligans in the neighborhood—better call the police. The last time I talked to my mother on the phone, she said, "This is the best one yet. The other day, your father said, 'What's the matter with us? We don't get along like we used to. Are you seeing someone else?'" My mother and I laughed together, but I think it's safe to say that her heart was breaking a little, too. She said, "I asked him, 'Have you seen my **wrinkles** lately?'"

It wouldn't matter if he didn't have macular degeneration and could see every line in her face. My father continues to adore my mother. Always has, always will. On every occasion that called for gifts, he lavished her with beautiful things: clothes, jewelry. On one memorable Christmas Eve, he gave her a full-length white mink coat. She didn't want it, but how could she tell him, him grinning and taking pictures of her wearing it as she stood next to the Christmas tree? She rarely wore it after that day, and when he asked why, she said, "It's too warm."

They kiss when they wake up in the morning, they kiss before they go to sleep. When my father worked, they kissed when he left and they kissed when he came home. He's a man whose mother died when he was around three years old, and he was raised by an emotionally bankrupt father and a cruel housekeeper. He found everything he needed in my mother, and that was always clear to me: she was his love. His pal. His partner. His confidante. His North Star. He does not want to be without her, not in the daytime and not at night. When I once suggested that my mother should probably have time away from him every now and then, he said, "I don't have much time left. The time I do have, why, I want to spend it with her."

My mother's views are somewhat different: when my parents stayed with me in a house where the guest room had twin beds, my mother exclaimed, "My own bed!" Her absolute delight was kind of heartbreaking.

Over twenty years ago, when my father had a heart attack, it was a whopper—his heart stopped twelve times in the ambulance on the way to the hospital, and at first it wasn't clear that he'd make it. I flew to Minnesota with a black dress in my suitcase, and went directly to his bedside. He was sleeping, surrounded by monitors, hooked up to IVs, pale in his hospital gown. When he opened his eyes, he said, "What are you doing here?"

"Oh, I was just in the neighborhood," I said, and he smiled. Then he said, "Where's your mother?"

I have heard this question all my life. It is like a brain tattoo, my father wanting to know where my mother is, because he wants her near him always.

These days, my mother says, he follows her around the house. She will say, "I'm going in to change the sheets," and he will come in the bedroom and watch her. She doesn't get out much, but she does have a standing weekly date to go shopping with her sisters. When that happens, he sits by the kitchen window, where there is a view of the street, to wait for her. She brings home his dinner; he will not eat without her. She worries about what will happen if he becomes more compromised, if she cannot leave him alone.

But my father's question, "Are you seeing someone else?" Oh, that was a good one. My mother later said, "You know, when I was in high school, I went out with Bob Harrington—I think we went to a powwow or something. And that was it. One date. I saw his obituary in the paper last week, and today your father said to me, 'You haven't been the same since you found out Bob died.'"

"Oh, God," I said, when she told me that. Tenderly.

It was on my mother's birthday when I spoke to her, and she said, "Your father felt so bad that he didn't get me a gift. And I told him, 'You know what you could give me for my birthday? Go in the den and do your Sudoku, or a crossword puzzle, or listen to one of your books on tape.'"

"Did he do it?" I asked.

"I don't think so," she said.

When my mother told me how bad my dad felt about not getting her a gift, I thought, **Whatever was I doing that would have been more important than taking my dad out to get his wife of sixty-seven years a birthday present?** I should have driven up from Chicago, or flown up, and taken my dad to the fanciest department store in town. I should have stood near him, guiding him as unobtrusively as I could; I should have said, "So whaddya think, Dad? What do you want to give her?" Apart from the full-on adoration you've given her since the day you met her. 1942. The back of the dime store. By the parakeets. You home on leave from the service. An introduction by a mutual friend.

Growing up with a father who was besotted with his wife lay down the gauntlet. I have not met the challenge. I failed in my marriage, and I have failed in relationships since, including the one I am in now; I fail a lot in the one I'm in now, but my partner, Bill, is patient. Sometimes I sit quietly to ponder why I have such trouble in relationships. "You just want to be free," an old boyfriend I'd run from told me when I saw him after many years. It was true then. I guess it still is, in a way. I want to be with someone and I want to be free, too. But sometimes I look at the fantastically outsized and romantic love I witnessed all my life between my parents and I think, **That's the reason. Who could measure up?**

NOVEMBER 28, 2010

Three cardinals on the black, bare branches of the tree just outside my window: nature's ornaments. Now that Thanksgiving is over, Christmas is unleashed like paper snakes from a cardboard can. There are plenty of reasons to despair over the gross commercialism of the holiday, but I confess to loving this time of year. I have put up my modest decorations, and I sit in the kitchen drinking coffee and looking at the little tree I have in that room as though it is Michelangelo's ceiling. I have the radio tuned to the Christmas station and tolerate every single song but the one by the Chipmunks.

For Thanksgiving, Bill and I visited my parents. I wanted to look in my father's eyes and see what I could see. So much about him was familiar to me, and unchanged: His blue eyes and the hair raked over his head and the still formidable width of his shoulders. His chuckle. His leaning forward to hear you better, his head slightly tilted, an expression of such earnestness, such willingness, on his face. The cucumbers and sour cream he makes and sprinkles liberally with paprika, stored in their usual spot on the second shelf of the refrigerator and covered with a shower cap, some freebie from a hotel that works just dandy and saves on the use of plastic wrap. His cache of pill bottles and Kleenex and small screwdriver and pad of paper and pencil (with T-shaped, two-headed eraser) in a basket at the side of the kitchen table.

But. "Do you want some wine?" he asked maybe fifteen times in the space of about half an hour, putting the question to Bill and to my mother, both of whom continued to patiently refuse. "I don't like red wine," my mother said. "I'm fine, Art," Bill said. Every time.

My father would sometimes tell a story about something I was quite certain did not happen, the type of story that was a reflection of a certain kind of paranoia that was taking hold, and I didn't know whether to interrupt and say, "Dad. That didn't happen. It seems like it did, but it didn't," or just sit quietly and listen to the exploits of the juvenile delinquents who like to do things like break into my father's car and sit in there. I elected to remain silent, but all the time I sat listening, a voice inside me was whispering to my father, **No, come back**.

On Thanksgiving afternoon, after I'd stuffed the turkey and put it in the oven, Bill and I took my father out to run errands, to give my mother some peace. It wasn't easy to get him to go. My father didn't want to leave my mom alone. She might need him to get something from the basement, he said. Or to take out the trash. Or something might happen to her. "What?" my mother said. "What might happen to me?" Here he drew himself up into what might be the best illustration of righteous indignation I will ever see, and began listing ominous possibilities: "She could fall" being primary among them. Finally, though, we convinced him to get into the car, and drove over to see his older brother Frank, who lives in a nursing home.

It can be a trial to visit such places, as everyone knows. The old people lined up in the hall in their wheelchairs, most sleeping, some staring vacantly ahead, some looking up hopefully at you as though you have come to rescue them. And in walking past them, you tell them you have not come to rescue them. And therefore it seems cruel to walk by them; it is hard to walk by them. "Hello!" I said, again and again, as kindly and cheerfully as I could, my meager compensation. "Hello!" to the woman clutching the teddy bear, to the man being held in a standing position by some sort of mechanical device that looked like it might have been used for medieval torture, to the one who startled awake from sleep with his neck at an odd angle and appeared completely bewildered by what he saw before him.

My mother doesn't like to go to this home; it depresses her, and of course I understand why. A few short years ago, I spoke to my uncle on the phone about his experiences in World War II. I was writing a novel that takes place during the war years, and I was looking for firsthand accounts of experiences in battle. Frank, who was living independently at the time, was generous in sharing all he could recall, including an incident where he was in the trenches and someone came to bring him dinner. He stood up to receive it, was shot in the chest by a sniper, went to the field hospital for treatment, and then went right back to the trenches. Never even told his fiancée, Ellen, that it happened. Ellen is long dead, but Frank looks for her, waits for her, wonders why she will not come to visit him. My sister tells me that this problem has gotten better since they took down pictures of Ellen, but it seems to me to be a heartbreaking solution, to trade staring at the lovely face of his bride and reliving memories of her for looking out the window at a view that is mostly parking lot. That is where we found him on Thanksgiving afternoon, sitting in his wheelchair and looking outside at the parking lot. He is quite deaf now; you must write on a board to communicate with him. The board and a marker are kept in a pocket on the back of his wheelchair, and there is also a harmonica there. I pulled the harmonica out, showed it to Frank, and he played a tune for his little audience, after which we gave him a round of applause. Then we were finished with that. I inquired after his son, and Frank told me he was fine. I asked if he was going to watch the football games that day and he shrugged in a positive way, as if he were saying, **Say, that wouldn't be a bad idea.** I reminded him about the three pieces of pecan and pumpkin and burgundy berry pie I'd brought him, and he said he'd eat them later and wasn't he lucky to have gotten them. When we left, he told us how grateful he was to have had visitors, and that he particularly liked seeing his brother, my dad. I wrote "We love you" on his board and he began to cry and then my dad began to tear up and I did, too. I stood a few feet away from the men as they embraced, and I watched them hold each other and thought about how many long years they'd been in each others' lives, and then I noticed I was holding my elbows and rocking side to side, as though I had a baby in my arms I was try-ing to comfort, and I made myself stand still. I looked away from the sight of those two old brothers (**Art! Art! Wake up! It's Christmas!**) and over to Frank's narrow closet door, on which was taped a construction paper ribbon of sorts; the shape of it was something like you might see on a pie at the county fair, and on it was written the fact that Frank was the recipient of two purple hearts. Exclamation point.

When we got outside, the sun was bright, and after everybody got in the car and put their seatbelt on, we drove off. And this seemed like a miracle all out of proportion to the fact. I know that sometimes when Frank asks my dad how he is, he answers, "Eh, I don't feel so good." To which Frank always raises an eyebrow and says, "You can walk around, can't you?"

Before we left, I asked the nurse if I might take Frank out to the lobby to watch the football game. "If you stay with him," she said. I told her we couldn't stay any longer—my father was anxious to get back home. "Oh, well, then, no," she said. "You can't leave him there alone." I didn't go back into Frank's room to tell him I couldn't set him up in front of the game in the lobby after all. I thought he had probably forgotten about my offer, and I didn't want to remind him of one more thing he couldn't do.

I knew Frank could watch the game on the little TV in his room, if he wanted to. It's just that I wanted to be fancier than that. In the lobby, you can see people come and go. You can watch them play cards or games, or help themselves to a cup of coffee. It's like flying first-class: you're still trapped, but at least there are some diversions. "Can I bring him some coffee?" I asked, and the nurse said no, he choked on liquids. "Oh," I said. "Good thing I asked you first." She smiled a little tiredly and I thought of her coming in her own front door after work, then settling herself down on the sofa, next to her hubby. I thought of him asking, "How was work?" and her answering, "Okay," then throwing an orange and brown afghan over her lap, and offering that same tired smile.

I had a talk with my dad before I left to go home. I told him he needed to make some effort to help himself, to try to engage in the world around him, to avail himself of some of the services that are there for people like him. The discussion got a little heated at one point, with my father putting up obstacles to virtually everything I suggested, and at one point laughing outright at me for one of those suggestions. And I came to tears over that. "Why are you **laughing** at me?" I said, which had more to do with old tapes than the situation at hand. (Old tapes: my need for his approval, for wanting always to please him first.) But he angrily threw out the fact that I live in Chicago and his son in Hawaii, we have deserted him, and too much falls to my sister, Vicki, who lives near them. I said something about the fact that he never seemed inclined to visit me in Chicago, despite numerous offers, and then I remembered I was dealing with someone who was compromised. I was picking on someone who could no longer have a rational discussion. So I reined myself in, lowered my voice, and told my father about a regular meeting of a small group of people who are dealing with memory loss. They meet twice a month to have conversations about various things, current events among them. There are speakers who come. There is singing, too, and there are crafts, although I didn't tell my dad that, because I thought a man who was once so mighty a figure would find it humiliating to be engaged in a sing-along or, oh, say, making a May basket using pipe cleaners woven into a blueberry container. But that's my own narrow-minded prejudice, my own sorrow at seeing a woman in Frank's nursing home sitting in the activities room and being helped to make a hand turkey, the kind that preschoolers hang up in their classrooms. Maybe it would be better to see my dad making a hand turkey than staring out the kitchen window at whatever he can still see and sighing.

"It's sad," my mother says. "He was a very intelligent man." But he asks her the same questions endlessly. Endlessly. "Has the mail come?" "Has the mail come?" "Did you bring in the mail yet?" "Has the mail come?" "Jeanne! Did the mail come?"

She tells me that every day when she gets up, she looks at herself in the bathroom mirror and asks God to give her patience. I think of their hearts banging in their chests on their wedding day, they way they couldn't wait to say yes to **in sickness and in health**.

About an hour after our discussion, my dad said, "I'm not mad, are you?" No, I said. "Truce?" he asked. "That depends," I said. "Truce if you promise me you'll try some things." "That's not a truce," he said.

But I got my dad to promise that he would try the group. I got him to promise that he would read one or two articles in the paper every day—I cut a few out for him when I was there, because we decided that it wouldn't be so hard to read a cut-out article under his magnifying machine—he wouldn't have to manipulate the large pages of the newspaper, or struggle with trying to find the continuation of stories; it would all be there before him.

My dad used to be an avid stamp collector, and I, like a lot of other people, always thought of it as a dippy hobby. But one day when I was visiting my parents, I looked through some of his albums, and many of the stamps were beautiful, miniature works of art. Others were like reading highly abbreviated synopses of historical events. So many pristine albums, all lined up on the shelves. He used to soak stamps off envelopes in a tiny dish of water. He used to handle them with tweezers. He used to order sheets of new stamps, and they would come in the mail and he would carefully mount them in the appropriate album. A few months ago, he sold a collection—the European one, I think it was—in order to help his grandson buy a house. He was a little unhappy about the price he got; he knew they were worth quite a bit more. This is in stark contrast to what he thinks his house is worth.

When we sat at the kitchen table talking about whether he and my mom should move to a place that offered assisted living, he asked, "How could we afford that?" And when I told him that, for starters, his house was worth over $200,000, he just looked at me a little sadly, as though it were a pity I was so out of touch with reality. "What did we pay for this house?" he asked my mother. "Twenty-two thousand," she said. "Well," he said, "we're not going to see much more than $24,000 for it."

I raised my hand. "Can I buy it?"

Sometimes, some things **are** funny.

Before I left my parents' house, I wanted to put a birdfeeder right outside the kitchen window, the kind that uses suction cups to adhere to the glass. But I learned they don't really work. And anyway, my father, a great bird lover, does still enjoy the parakeets my sister and I bought him. Every night, he says, "Good night, Fritzi. Good night, Frieda." And every morning, when he takes the towel off their cage, there they are, still alive, and eager to eat whatever gets put into their cup. "Good morning, Fritzi," he says. "Good morning, Frieda." Reveille.

Also, every morning, my father makes sure his hair is combed and the collar of his bathrobe lies flat and neat before he makes an appearance in the kitchen, where he greets my mother and gives her a kiss. (When I was there, he was sitting in the booth and eating breakfast beside my mother one morning, and a look of great concern came over his face. He turned to her and said, "Did I kiss you this morning?" "Yes," she said. He kissed her again anyway.)

The other day, I read something about William Blake, about how when he lay on his deathbed, he told his wife to hold very still, he wanted to make a drawing of her, "for you have ever been an angel to me." He made her portrait, and then he began to sing, and then he died. I read that, and I began to cry. But I am newly home from a visit to the front, and a lot of things are making me cry: a late bud on the hydrangea bush, a rosy dawn, the memory of how, on Thanksgiving night, my father sat alone in the kitchen working to get a battery in his hearing aid.

The battery is small and his hands are large. He can't see well at all, of course. My sister was sitting beside me at the dinner table, and we could see him out in the kitchen and we both watched him for a while. "It's hard to get those things in," she said, and we watched a little more, hoping that he could secure for himself this small victory, but then, finally, she went to help him.

I think of getting up early every day when I was at my parents' house to sit quietly alone in the living room just to look at how things are arranged: the candy dish on the coffee table, the sheer draperies on the brass rings before the bay window, the lamps positioned perfectly for reading next to chairs, the little desk against the wall, its chair pushed neatly beneath it. I listened those mornings to the grandfather clock ticking and I felt the reverberations of its deep chime right at the center of my chest, like another heart.

But mostly I try to think of something my father said this last visit: "I had a lot of good times in my life." He said it twice.

Yesterday, I mailed him two stamps I got from the envelope of a fan letter a man sent me from Australia. Last night, Bill and I found two articles in the paper to send my father. One was from the business section of **The New York Times**, a funky story about a woman in Atlanta trying to sell her very successful eight-seat hamburger joint. She sells the best burgers in town, using a secret recipe that she says she'll share only with the new owner. She wants to sell, she says, so that she can take a nap.

The other article was about the leader of the free world getting his lip split in a basketball game. I love Obama; my dad hates him. I thought it would cheer him up to see that my hero had been hurt.

I came home to a message on my phone from my mother. "Well, I got my book," she said, referring to the large-print novel I'd sent her. "So at least one good thing happened today." Then she listed the not-so-good things that had happened: the wife of a cousin of mine had died, after a long battle with cancer during which she complained never. And her sister, Tish, had fallen on the ice and broken her arm, so she would not be able to drive for some time. That meant that she couldn't take my mother and their other sister, Lala, out for their weekly expeditions: usually, a visit to the dollar store or Unique Thrift Shop or Herberger's department store. Then they have lunch out at someplace like Snuffy's

Malt Shop. Occasionally they go to a movie, where they hold hands and guide themselves down the dark aisle with a flashlight my mother keeps in her purse, and where my Aunt Lala usually falls asleep—hard to stay interested in a movie when your macular degeneration has progressed to the point where you can't really see the film.

The third piece of bad news was that my father, after having agreed to attend a meeting of the group dealing with memory loss, refused to go after all. "Why won't you go?" my mother asked, and he said, "I don't feel good." So he stayed home, and I assume he continued his pattern of following my mother anywhere in the house she went.

I called her back and there was such weariness in her voice. But she is the daughter of an optimistic Irishman who loved life, and I could hear her trying to rally, even as we spoke. She put me on the phone with my father and I asked him rather sharply why he didn't go to the group. "Didn't feel good," he said. And I said, "Dad."

My mother got back on the phone with me before I hung up, and I said, "I yelled at Dad a little bit." "Oh, that won't help," she said, and what was in her voice was compassion for her husband of now sixty-eight years—their anniversary was January 15.

In January 1943, my mother rode a train from St. Paul, Minnesota, to an Army base in Texas, where she married my father. Her mother did not want her to do it. She didn't like my dad; she said he had too much hair. Naturally I assume there were other things about him that she didn't like, but what she told my mom was that my dad had too much hair. My mom wore a yellow dress and a brown velvet hat to get married in. Her maid of honor was a first lieutenant. Their honeymoon cottage was the top floor of a rooming house someone rented out to them, and there were complaints about the, ahem, noise they made at night. My sister was born nine months later.

Yesterday, that sister called, and when I asked her how things were going with my parents, she sighed and said, "One day at a time." We talked about how difficult it is for my parents to navigate the stairs in their house—down to the basement, up to the attic. We talked about how transportation to the many (and ever-increasing) doctors' appointments are a problem, because my parents must scramble around for rides. I bought them a gift certificate for a car service two Christmases ago, but they rarely use it. It's like the beautiful negligees my father used to give my mother, gossamer things in colors of pale blue or apricot or cream that she would lift partway out of the box and then hastily cover with the tissue paper they lay nestled in. Once, when I was a teenager and my parents were out and I was searching for my as yet unwrapped Christmas gifts, I found the drawer in my mother's dresser where she kept those negligees. They were neatly folded, still in their tissue paper. I don't know that she ever wore them. That's how they treat the car service.

I told my sister I worried about them eating well, about the way neither one of them is able to get out and socialize, about what would happen if one of them fell. "And you know what?" I said. "All of those things would be taken care of it they'd just move to that place we showed them. A bus would take them to their doctors. A bus would take Mom to church. There are activities every day: field trips, lectures, crafts, movies. If Mom doesn't want to cook, they could go to the dining room. There are people to talk to. There's a little library Mom could go to; there's a breakfast club for the men. There's a community garden. In the winter, they could come out of their apartment and go for a walk without even having to go outside! And!" I said, practically sputtering in my self-righteous eagerness. "Dad could keep his car in a heated garage!"

"I know," my sister said.

"I mean, I think we have to get a little **tough** with them!" I said. "Mom needs a break. If Dad 'doesn't feel good,' let him go sit in a group of people talking about current events and not feel good. I bet he'd feel better just by being around other people!"

"He says it's easier to meet people as a couple," my sister said. "He wants her to come with him."

"That group is so she can get a break from **being** with him all the time," I said. "And so that Dad can meet someone besides Mom to talk to."

"I was going to talk to them tomorrow," my sister said. "I was going to sit them down and say, 'Look. You're going to have to make

some decisions. You aren't safe here anymore.' I was going to tell Dad that Mom is
stressed to the max; she can't keep caring for
him this way."

"Right!" I said. "If he loves her so much,
he needs to make things a little easier for
her, even if it makes him uncomfortable. Do
you want me to drive up and talk to them
with you?"

"No," she said. "Let me see how this goes."

"Call me if you need me," I said, and she
said okay.

I sat fuming for a while, thinking of how
at this point it's just selfish of my dad not
to try to help himself. My mother makes the
calls, she has people come over to evaluate
my dad, she gets everything all set up, and
then he won't go. When he says, "I don't feel
good," what he's saying is, "You come, too."
Selfish!

I worked myself into a nice state of anger,
and had fantasies of putting my dad in my
car and driving him over to the assisted living
place, shoving him into a nice little apartment, then throwing his things in the door
after him, his grandfather clock and his car-
digan sweaters and his hearing aids and his

wire basket full of golf balls. And then I felt a guilty rush of sorrow, because I know it's hard for them to leave their home with its arched doorways and cozy kitchen, with its history of so many Christmas and Easter dinners, with memories of grand-children who first came to that house as in-fants and now have children of their own. My mother's mother lived in the room that is now the TV room; my brother had a room in the basement, complete with a pretty well-stocked bar. My parents are deeply familiar with their house; if the lights went out, they could find their way around. The beautiful bay window, the little backyard in which my mother loves to putter with her flowers, the nearness to Como Park, my father's work-bench and watchmaker's cabinet and stack of **National Geographic**s in the basement.

Last night I went to the symphony. I had seen an ad for music by Mozart at the Chicago Symphony Orchestra, and felt a surge of longing to go; then I realized I **could** go.

I remember being nine years old, lying on my stomach in my bedroom next to the record player and listening to a record of

Chopin piano music. I don't know where it came from—the library, maybe. But listening to it, I got a feeling that was nearly painful. I remember, too, going with my parents to have dinner at my Uncle Frank's house, and I would leave the table of chattering adults and go to sit at his piano and make chords. Then I put my foot to the sustain pedal so that the sound would last and last. I wanted to take piano lessons, but we had no piano. I wanted to know all about classical music, but I never did learn much about it.

So. I bought a ticket to the Chicago Symphony Orchestra. In the cab on the way there, the driver (who wore a red shirt and a kind of Elvis hairdo and a pinkie ring) asked me in an accent I couldn't identify where I was headed. "To the symphony," I said. "I'm going to hear a little Mozart."

"Ah," he said. "Yes. You listen to the music and relax. You forget about your worries and all the cares of the world."

"Right," I said.

"You know what music is the most relaxing?" he asked. "They've done studies. You know what's the most relaxing music to the human spirit? Indian. Not American Indian, East Indian."

"The Beatles were onto something," I said, and he said yes, they were.

I arrived early enough to hear part of a lecture about the music we were about to hear, and the room where the lecture was held was so beautiful it was a little hard to pay attention. I kept imagining someone getting married there: a violinist and a percussionist, she Asian and a lover of flourless chocolate cake, he a blond-headed boy from Iowa who practiced drums in the barn. But then the lecturer played a little bit of a soprano singing a Mozart aria. And I swooned. At the end of the lecture, the man asked for questions. I wanted to know who the soprano was, but I was embarrassed to ask. I figured everyone else would know; I figured they'd turn in their seats to see the country bumpkin who got let in here. So as everyone was filing out, I went up to the lecturer and asked, "Who was the soprano?" He got a blank look and then said, "Oh! That was Natalie Dessay. French. She's wonderful." I made a note to myself to buy her CDs.

I went out to the lobby and bought myself a bottle of Pellegrino, drank it down, and then headed for my seat, right in the center on the main floor, eight rows back. I could practically see the hair on the knuckles of the bass players, which was not particularly useful, because much of the time I closed my eyes to hear the music better. I sat in a line of three women, all of us unaccompanied. The woman next to me closed her eyes, too, but then she began gently snoring. Never mind; she was no competition to the full sound of the orchestra, to the piano played with such passion by Mitsuko Uchida, who was also conducting.

Periodically, I opened my eyes to watch the musicians, and I also watched a couple ahead of me. They were an older couple, probably in their mid-eighties, and when the man needed to stand to make way for people going to seats past his own, he had great difficulty getting up. His wife had to help him, and it took quite a while. She was giving him quiet but urgent instructions: **Walter, hold on! Hold on to the armrest! Now stand up!** He stood, and I saw that he was a very tall man, with broad shoulders and a still handsome face. He was well dressed: a tweed suit, a Burberry scarf, a camel-colored cashmere coat draped behind him. After he stood, the coat slid down into his seat, and was lumpy behind him. I wanted to straighten it, but I didn't want to embarrass him.

We listened to Piano Concerto No. 11 in F Major, and I saw how this couple sat so close together, shoulder pressed into shoulder. We listened to Divertimento in B-flat Major, and by then he had his arm around her. During the intermission that followed, he moved slowly, carefully, to the end of the aisle, where no one else had sat, and where it would be easier for him to get out when the concert was over. But I could see them well, including the soft curls along the side of her face when she turned to look at him, which was often.

During the second half of the concert, we heard Piano Concerto No. 21 in C Major, known to many because it was used to great effect in the sixties film **Elvira Madigan**. During the Allegro maestoso, I saw Walter pat his wife's arm, as though in consolation: **There, there: listen!**

The concert was a huge success: the

orchestra received a standing ovation. As people stood enthusiastically applauding, I saw Walter's wife unfold a walker and help him into his coat. She got him positioned for the long walk up the aisle, and then there they went. He moved very slowly, but he moved, and as he and his wife passed by me, I saw what I thought was the peace of the music in their faces.

Three times, the conductor was called back to take her bows. She stood in triumph upon the stage, her hand over her heart, and dipped down, over and over again. Walter and his wife walked slowly, slowly up the aisle, it seemed literally inch by inch. From here and there in the audience came exuberant cries of "Bravo!" "Bravo!" I know those cries were not for Walter and his wife. But in my mind, I made them be.

JANUARY 30, 2011

I woke up this morning with a moral hangover.

Last night, my sister called to tell me that she had taken my parents to a facility that has independent living, assisted care, and a "memory center." So if you are living with someone who gets Alzheimer's, he or she can be moved, when the time comes, to a building that is connected to your own, and you can visit them anytime, without even going outside.

"So how did it go?" I asked.

"Dad liked it," she said. "He said, 'I would live here.'"

"Really!" I said.

"And Mom said she wanted a two-bedroom, but all that's available now is a one-bedroom."

"They could take that and then move when a two-bedroom opened up," I said, and she said, "Well, exactly. I told them to talk it over, but they should decide soon, because those places go fast. They don't even advertise."

My sister told me about the various things she and my parents had seen: the apartment itself, the dining room, the library, the little on-site grocery store, the solarium. She said my father would be allowed to ride his mobility scooter there; she said there were cribbage games going on all the time that he might like to go to.

My sister also said that in the car on the way over, Dad said his parakeets talk, but they stop whenever anyone comes into the room. They talk the way **people** talk, he meant—intentionally, conversationally, not imitatively. "They speak very well," he said. "What do they talk about?" my mother asked, and my father said, "I don't know."

My sister also said that our father is

continuing to have paranoid fantasies that someone is looking in his windows, especially the bedroom windows, and that it might make him feel better to be up higher, as he would be if they moved. She said she tries to tell him that these things are only in his mind, but when she does, he gets mad. "And then his cheek starts going, you know," she said and I thought, **Yeah, I know.** I remember that cheek going in and out. I will never forget it. It happened when he got mad; it was what you saw before he yelled at you or hit you or both. It's funny how a phrase like **his cheek starts going** brings it all back, that feeling I had of something caged and weighty in my chest, and the chronic despair that came with it, the feeling that I would never be out from under that kind of fear, not only of him, but of the world.

When I was in my mid-thirties and had two children of my own, I finally confronted him. I told him I'd been scared of him all my life, and that I had not one memory of him ever saying he loved me or was proud of me, and he was so surprised. He was surprised! And after that day, things changed between us, so much so that he and I became very close, and it was hard to reconcile the way he used to be with the way he was now.

And here we are at a new now, my dad and my mom and my sister and me. I awakened today feeling like a bully, feeling like I am forcing my parents to do something that will break their hearts. I lay in bed in gray light imagining my father coming into the kitchen this morning to sit in the banquette opposite his wife. I imagined him saying, "So?" and her only nodding. Wanting, perhaps, to cry, but only nodding. Their world has narrowed so; their options are so few. As much as they may dislike it, surely they must see that the most practical way for them to carry on— the only **safe** way for them to carry on—is for them to make this move. They know they don't need to do anything but go over and try it for a couple of months; it rents month-to-month. They know I'll pay for it, and that they need not sell their house, that they can rent furniture and just bring clothes and a few other things and try it out. If they hate it, they can come back home, and it will be spring and my mother's tulips will be com-ing up in the garden. I guess it's unlikely

that they would come back, though. I guess
that's what they imagine, too. You set foot in
a certain kind of river and you know that as
soon as you do, the current will have you.
I'm so sorry, I want to tell them. But I also
want to tell them what I've heard happens so
many times: people are dragged kicking and
screaming into these kind of places, and then
they end up loving them and saying they
should have moved there years ago. Still, **I'm
so sorry**, I want to say. But this is the time
for me to say nothing. This is the time for me
to simply wait and let them decide what they
want to say.

It is twelve noon on a Sunday. I am still
in my pajamas. I read the paper this morning. I made blueberry buttermilk pancakes
and pepper bacon for breakfast. While I was
cleaning up afterward, I noticed my dog,
Homer, sitting by the back door, staring in-
tently out. That door, which is mostly glass,
is his television. He watches for squirrels in
the yard, he watches the birds at the feeder,
he monitors the comings and goings of my
neighbors. "What are you looking at, pal?"
I asked him. He looked quickly over at me,
then away; he didn't want to be disturbed. I

sat down on the floor beside him and put my arm around him. We sat there for some time, looking out together at the falling snow, the red cardinals, the swift flight of the rabbits who see something that scares them and run away to safety.

FEBRUARY 9, 2011

When I was growing up and my military family was living in the states and not overseas, we used to come "home" to Minnesota for a couple of weeks every summer. (As an Army brat, I never really felt I had a home anywhere, but Minnesota was the place my parents came from, and where their siblings lived. Close enough.) Whenever we visited, we three kids would get split up, and in the early years I would stay with my Aunt Lala, she of legendary cleanliness and excellent meatloaf and nightly washups in the kitchen sink using a big metal pan and Ivory soap, and don't even think about skipping your ears. I remember once coming to Aunt Lala's late at night and being shown to a bed she had fixed up for me with sheets that smelled like leaves and the wind; I remember I lay there with the fabric over my nose, thinking I was so happy to be out of the car and here in this place with the toilet with the chain pull and the wooden columns that separated the living room from the dining room and the five children who lived here and were my cousins. I remember Lala's husband, Roy, whose nickname was French, and how his extreme handsomeness always made me a little nervous: black curly hair, a chiseled face with high cheekbones, a dimple in his chin. I remember standing by Aunt Lala in the basement, watching her use her terrifying wringer washer, and how she told me you had to be careful not to break the buttons when you put the shirts and blouses through the moving rollers that squeezed the water out. Had to watch your fingers, too.

I remember neighborhood kids coming to the backyard, and the way that, rather than knocking on the door, they called out the name of the person they wanted. So you might hear, decrescendo, **Ohhhhh, Diannnne**, and then the cousin I hung around with the most would bang out the screen door to play with her friends, and she would let me, the shy interloper, come, too. Once, a friend of hers whispered, "Can't you ditch her?" and Diane said no. I am grateful to this day.

When I was fifteen, I began staying instead with Aunt Tish, described by her son Tim as the world's oldest teenager. Tish had a great zest for life, an abiding curiosity, and unmatched generosity, which translated to a kind of general willingness. She also had a great sense of humor, which I enjoyed tremendously, except for the time she made fun of my Simon and Garfunkel album, insisting on calling the duo Simon and Garfinkle, just to get under my melodramatic skin (I who lay on her living room floor mooning over my faraway boyfriend and listening to "Kathy's Song" over and over). Tish was the kind of person who could draw little kids out, asking a five-year-old, for example, "Do you have a girlfriend?" If the answer was no, she'd say, "Oh. So no plans for marriage yet, huh?" She used to eat ice cubes while she lay out in the sun on her chaise lounge, tanning, even though her dentist had told her chewing on those things would ruin her teeth. She was a wonderful cook, and she made things like monkey bread, which I loved both for its name and its taste. Her late husband, my uncle Bob, was nuts about her. Tish was engaged to another man when Bob met her—Bob had come back from the war to the insurance company where she worked, and, in the accepted way of the times, she was training him to take her job. After a week of working together, my uncle left a note on her desk that said, "You don't know it yet, young lady, but one day you're going to marry me." Eight months later, she did.

Once, when I was staying there, Tish and Bob went to the movies to see **My Fair Lady.** When they came home, Tish ascended the staircase in a pseudo-dramatic fashion, saying she was going to bed to dream about Rex Harrison. I saw Uncle Bob standing at the foot of the stairs looking after her with what I believed was a kind of simmering jealousy that he knew was ridiculous but was there just the same. But then, everyone loved Tish; everybody wanted to be the one she focused her attention on. She was the kind of person who offered you a safe landing, no matter what you said to her. And she was interested in you in a non-phony way, whether you were a five-year-old or a ninety-year-old. She was interested in just about everything. Once, as she lay out on her chaise on a warm summer night, she looked up at the stars and said to her sixteen-year-old son, "Tell me about the stars, Tim," and he didn't roll his eyes in that teenager way; instead, he did what his mother asked him to. He opened with "Well, the sun is a star," and when she said, **"Really?!"** he seemed to grow an inch right before my eyes.

My mother was always close to her five sisters; now she has two left. For some time they relied on Tish to get them out and about, since she was the only one who could drive anymore—though, as her daughter, Patty, has said, she would never make a left turn when three right turns would do. But then Tish fell and broke her arm. She had surgery for it on Tuesday. She sailed through the operation, a great feat for a woman who's eighty-six years old, and we were all so relieved. Then, the next day, she had a stroke. She had surgery again to clear a carotid artery, and a brain scan afterward yielded positive results. (**Awesome results,** was the way the doctor described it.) Tish was having some problems breathing, though, and after a lengthy discussion with her children, she was moved to intensive care and put on a ventilator. When I heard this news, I paced around and around my house. Then I called Amtrak and got tickets to go . . . well, home. I wanted to see Tish, and I figured that, while I was there, my sister and I could go with our parents to see the facility where we thought they should move. The appointment was for the next day.

The train I took left the station four hours late. In the waiting area, there was a greatly pregnant woman. She lay sprawled in her chair, her top raised to expose her belly, and she slathered lotion on it again and again. She also spoke loudly, saying repeatedly to anyone who cared to listen, "I'm so tired! I'm due **any day**!" I don't think I was alone in worrying that she would deliver onboard. She was traveling with two young children who were extremely well behaved, a boy and girl aged maybe four and six, and they were a study in how to pass the time. They ignored the mindless shows on the television, which was turned up much too loudly and served as the auditory equivalent of stale cigarette smoke. Instead, they quietly played with each other, making up fantasy games and never complaining about how ridiculous this delay was. The pregnant woman was also traveling with a markedly overweight female companion who, after listening to her complain for an hour or so, pointedly went to sleep, her head back, her mouth gaping open.

I'd been scheduled to arrive at 10:30 that night, so after I finally got myself settled on the train, I called my mother and told her not to wait up for me—we were going to be a good four hours late. At three-thirty in the morning, I was asleep on the train when my cellphone rang. "Where **are** you?" my mother said, and I said, "What are you doing up? I told you to go to bed!" "But where **are** you, though?" she asked, and I looked out the train window and said, "I don't know." The train was not moving. I had a little conversation with the man across the aisle, who told me there'd been some incident and the police had closed the tracks for six miles in either direction. No one knew when we'd move again. I told my mother I'd be there sometime in the morning, to go to bed. Then, seeing the car attendant, I asked him what was going on. He acted very mysterious and self-important and repeated the fact that the police had closed the tracks. "But why?" I asked, and he said, "That's all we know," but it seemed clear to me that he was lying. I called the police in the town we were closest to, and they knew nothing. I called the state police and they knew nothing. The train attendant passed by again and I said, "Hey, Jeremy, are you nervous at all?" "No," he said, and so I went back to sleep. At eight-thirty in the morning, the train pulled into the station, ten hours late. At nine in the morning, the cab I took pulled up to my parents' house, and I had breakfast with them and told them all about my great adventure. I'd found out that a freight train had hit someone.

A few hours later, my sister and I took my parents to the facility to look at a two-bedroom unit that had opened up: a man I'll call Ted had a wife who had moved to the Alzheimer's unit and he was downsizing to a one-bedroom that had just become available. On the door leading out to the hall was a note Ted had written to his wife asking her please not to leave the apartment, to come and wake him up if he was sleeping or to knock on the door if he was in the bathroom and he would come and help her. At the end of the note was written, **I love you.**

There was a wonderful view of woods and a stream from all the windows of the place, and Ted told us, "You can watch the salmon spawning." Ha, ha, we said, but it lifted everyone's spirits, it seemed, to be in a place where there were a lot of people my parents might be able to make friends with, or at least talk to. In the exercise room, my sister tried one of the machines, and then my dad did, too, and I thought, **Hallelujah**. In the lobby, I spoke with three women who were hanging around and asked them how the food was there. One offered the hand gesture that means "so-so." I asked if they liked living there and was met with a much more enthusiastic response. Oh yes, they all said, they really did. I asked one of the women how long she'd been there, and she consulted the ceiling and then allowed as how she wasn't exactly sure. Nor was another of the three sure how long she'd been there. The third answered exactly how long she'd been there with some measure of pride. Then they all laughed. I thought, **Good. My dad will be fine here**.

On Sunday, my parents' house was given over to repair and redecorating. There was a major plumbing problem that my sister's husband and son labored all day to fix. I gave my dad's birds' cage a cleaning like they'd never seen, something that only someone far from home and absent the list of normal obligations would do. Then Vicki and I tore into my parents' TV room, pulling out furniture and vacuuming up birdseed and feathers, and reversing the placement of the television and the reading machine so that they could hear and see the TV better. We made them come in and try it out and were pleased when they both said, "Oh, sure, this is much better."

That evening was the Super Bowl. My cousin Chris, who is Lala's youngest son and who lives with her in her modest house to serve as her caretaker, invited us to watch the game and to have dinner there. So I brought my parents over and we enjoyed Chris's hospitality: he met us outside and helped walk my parents across the street, then moved the car so that they wouldn't have to cross the street again on the way out. When we settled ourselves on the sofa and chairs, he offered appetizers of SunChips and slices of cheese neatly laid out on a platter. Beer anyone? Wine? After a little while, we moved to the little dining room for a dinner of beef Stroganoff ("It's from a box," Chris said, "but it's good, isn't it?") and corn and salad. For dessert: cheesecake with strawberry sauce. Coffee, anyone? Cream?

At dinner, I was sitting next to Bill, Chris's brother, who is closest to my age and is the other one of Lala's children with whom I played when I stayed with them, and I looked at his profile and superimposed upon it was his profile from when he was just a kid. I thought back then that he was the funniest person on the face of the earth. He used to crack me up with his made-up stories about Mrs. Peabody and Mrs. McGillicuddy, and I stood in awe, watching, whenever he lay on his belly to dash off one of his drawings of fighter planes, bullets flying all around it.

When our parents got together at the house where French and Lala used to live, all of us cousins used to pile up on a sofa on the big screened-in front porch and happily punch and tickle each other for what seemed like hours. Inside, on the tiny black-and-white television set, the fights were on, and Hamm's beer commercials played between rounds: Indian drumming was the background to the song, which went **From the land of sky blue waters . . .** There was always a huge bakery box of donuts in the kitchen, and we would take turns doing runs for more, more, more treats.

I sat at the dining room table remembering all this as I looked over at my cousin, and finally I said, "Hey, Bill, isn't this just like old times?"

"Yeah," he said, and laughed, and in it was affection but irony, too, for the way that **Oh my goodness, things have changed**, for the way that so many things have happened to us cousins. Marriages and divorces. Births of children and deaths of children. A suicide. Success in jobs and failure at jobs. A kind of wild optimism that was in all of us that has eroded as it must with the tired realities of life, with the anvil of aging that has fallen on our parents and will fall on us, too, should we live that long.

After dinner, we adjourned to the living room again to watch the game in earnest. My dad had a chair pulled up close to the TV to see the little he could, Lala chatted with her guests because she couldn't see much of anything, and I watched for a while, but then, failing as usual to understand one single thing about the game, I sat at the dining room table looking at photo albums I'd asked if I might see. A lot of the old photos had been given away, but I found a few of them at the back of one of the albums, and I sat looking at my aunts and uncles as people far younger than I was now. Bill wandered over and looked at the photos with me for a while, then told me to come with him. He led me into his mother's bedroom to show me a photo hung on the wall, one of Lala that French had carried during the war. "Didn't she look like Rita Hayworth, though?" Bill said, and I nodded, my heart in my throat, as we stood side by side before that image, staring at it. And then I just looked at Bill and I saw that he knew everything I was feeling because he was feeling it, too. We went back out to the living room and watched the end of the game, and I paid off my debt to my parents: five dollars I'd bet on the team that lost.

On Monday, we went to the hospital to visit Tish in the ICU. I let my mother go in alone first, and I saw how she bent forward and stroked her sister's hand and spoke softly, musically, to her. I saw Tish's legs move; it was as though she was excited to see her sister. I stood out in the hall with Tish's daughter, Patty, who said, "My mom's probably going to be mad as hell that we let them put that tube down, but it seemed like the best decision." It was thought that Tish would come off the vent in a day or so and then start a rehab process that was going to be a bit lengthy but would lead to a complete recovery. Which I reinforced, as instructed, when it was my turn to see Tish. "Hey," I said, "you know what? You're only going to have that dang thing in your throat another day or so and then you'll be on your way to being a chauffeur again." She looked up at me and it seemed to me she was trying to speak;

there was a little movement in her throat, but mostly she just looked up at me with her storm-blue eyes, and I thought about an extremely hot summer day I was staying with her, how it was really too hot to eat and so she made fruit salad for dinner, and when Bob came home and asked what was for dinner and she told him fruit salad, he said, **"Fruit salad?!"** and put on his hat and left the house. Tish said he was probably going to go out to get a steak at O'Gara's, so the rest of us sat down and enjoyed her fruit salad with whipped cream quite a bit; everything that woman made in the kitchen was **good**. I was going to share that memory with Tish, but I figured I'd do it later, when she could laugh and say something irreverent about Bob. So I just said, "Everybody loves you so much." Then I said I'd see her later and I came back out in the hall and hugged Patty goodbye.

In the car, my mom said she'd told Tish that there was no way they were going to open that new dollar store without her; the sisters' old dollar store had closed but a new one was opening even closer to my mom's house, right near the Rainbow grocery store, where Tish took my mom shopping regularly. Every time they went, Tish forbade my mother from buying pinwheel cookies because they were too expensive, but she didn't mind at all sharing in the winnings of the scratch-away betting card she always convinced my mother to buy.

After the visit to Tish, my mom and I picked up my father and we all went out to see his brother Frank at the nursing home. Sometimes it's hard to come up with conversation; Frank's short-term memory is completely shot, as is his hearing. At one point, I wrote on his communication board, **What's an escape wheel?**

In a book I'd read recently, I'd come upon the phrase "the escape wheel of the going train" and knew it referred to parts of a clock but no more than that. Frank used to be a watchmaker, as was my dad, after he retired from the Army; for many years, he and Frank co-owned a jewelry and watch repair shop. When I asked Frank what that term meant, his face lit up and he painstakingly described the gear and its function, and then drew it, to boot. "Ah," I said, "I understand," though I did not, not completely. It was not because the explanation was not fine; it was because

I have trouble understanding such things, though clearly Frank does not.

Here is what the whole phrase means: the **escape wheel** is a toothed wheel for regulating a going train to which it is geared, engaging intermittently with the pallets of a pendulum or balance mechanism in such a way as to cause the mechanism to oscillate rhythmically and, in so doing, free the going train for part of each oscillation. The **going train** is the gear train for moving the hands of the timepiece or giving some other visual indication of the time. Even as I write this, I still don't understand much beyond the lyricism, the buried poetry of those words. And for the way they seem to somehow serve as metaphor for the situation at hand.

We had brought some Valentine cookies for Frank that my sister had gotten for him— shortbread with pink sugar crystals—and he dove into them with relish. It seemed like he was in a good mood. We left the home feeling pretty happy, and my sister came in to meet us for dinner, which was pizza that Vicki and I volunteered to pick up. She and I relish the time away from our parents, so we can gossip about them, and I always imagine that at such times our parents gossip about Vicki and me. I know my dad thinks we're interfering too much in his life. Once he waved his hand impatiently at me and said, "Your mother and I have been together for a long time, we love each other, we'll work this out." I switched to passive assertive to answer: "Yes. It will be worked out."

On the Tuesday morning before I left, I sat in the kitchen booth and had breakfast with my parents. About ten minutes after my dad finished his cereal, he said, "What's to eat around here?" My mother and I looked at each other. She told my father, "You just ate." "What?" he said, and leaned in closer to hear. "You **just ate**!" she said, and he shrugged in a way that seemed to say, **If you say so**. "You had **cereal**," she told him, and he said, "Okay." My mother's face softened, and she said, "If you're hungry, I'll feed you," and I died one of those little deaths. "No," he said. "Never mind," and then I died another one.

I got out the newspaper and the three of us tried to complete that morning's crossword puzzle. My mom got a few words, I got a few, and my dad got a couple. All together, though, we did poorly. If I were to give us a grade, it would be a D. After about fifteen minutes, I pushed the newspaper away, saying, "This is too hard," and my parents kind of looked at each other and I imagined they were thinking, **You want to know about "too hard"?** and I loved that they had that moment of sharing something together. I loved that I was excluded from it, that it was theirs alone, that they were aligned on that side of the table, together.

When I got to the airport, I sat in a chair and checked my phone for emails. There weren't any. But I kept checking and checking, wanting to be back at home before I got there.

On Wednesday, my mother left another message on my phone, and she sounded very pleased: **Well, good news. She's off the vent, and the first thing Tish said when Patty visited was "They took it** out." **They moved her out of ICU and down to the medical floor. Oh, and there was a Valentine's Day party at Frank's nursing home, and they elected a king and a queen. Frank is king.**

When I checked my email later, I saw that
Vicki had sent me a photo of Frank in his re-
galia. There he was, sitting in his wheelchair,
a blue blanket pulled up high over him, wearing his royal crown and his royal robe. Vicki
told me he didn't really seem to know what
was going on, but then neither did the queen.
In the picture, Frank was smiling; he seemed
happy. The crown was actually a very nice
one, and it sat high and straight upon his
head. The red robe with the white fur collar lay smoothly on his shoulders, and in his
hand was a kind of scepter: a red velvet rose.
Long-stemmed. Beautiful, in spite of itself.

On Thursday evening, I was making Thai let-
tuce wraps for dinner. There's a lot of vegetables in them, and I like chopping to music,
so I had the stereo turned up loud: Duffy's
new CD. I was in a bit of a hurry because Bill
was due home in about twenty minutes and
I was far from finished. So when the phone
rang, I answered it impatiently. I heard my
mother's voice saying my name and it was
very soft and tremulous.

"Mom?" I said.

"Sad news," she said, weeping. "Tish is dying."

"What?" I said. **"What?"**

"She's back up in ICU on the ventilator again. They're just keeping her on it until we can get there to say goodbye."

"But what happened?" I asked, and my mother told me as much as she knew, which was that Tish started having some sort of breathing problem, and . . . and . . . She said she couldn't talk more; she had to go. "Oh, Mom, I'm so sorry," I said, and she said she'd call me later.

I stood frozen in the kitchen, the knife in my hand. Then I started crying, and then I went back to chopping. When Bill came in the door, he called my name and I said, "Yes?" and he said, "Are you okay?" and I said no and I told him what happened and I kept on crying and chopping, crying and chopping. He asked, gently, if I wanted to not make dinner and I said no, we would eat. And then, I said, in the morning I was going back to Minnesota. I would drive and I would take my new puppy, Gabby, because I didn't know when the funeral would be and I thought it

was most important that I be there now before the funeral. I kept wondering how my
dad would react, if he could give my mother
room for what was going to be a profound
grief, if he could comfort her. I felt someone needed to be there. "Yes, okay, I'll take
care of things here," Bill said. I ate dinner.
I packed. I called my mother and told her I
was coming. She had been at the hospital to
say goodbye. She said she had sung her sister
a song. "What did you sing?" I asked. "Well,"
she said, "I sang, **Hush, little baby, don't
you cry.** That's what I sang to Becky when
she died." Becky was my mother's youngest sister, the first of five sisters who died, a
number of years ago. When Becky knew she
wasn't going to make it, she said, "Well, I
didn't think I'd be the last to die, necessarily,
but I sure didn't think I'd be the first."

Tish had no opportunity to make any
such pronouncements, of course, because her
death was such a surprise. A puzzlement. A
black event that had all of us saying the word
that is a reflex in such situations: **"What?"**
After my mother told me about how she sang
goodbye to Tish, she said, "Ah, me. Another
chapter closed."

I told my mother again how very sorry I was, and that I'd see her tomorrow. She expressed some worry about my driving alone and I said it would be no problem, there was no weather to worry about between here and there. In truth, I had no idea about this. But I thought if I ran into anything, I'd figure out what to do then. Sit in a Motel 6 and watch out the window for things to change. Whatever.

I went to bed and I lay in the darkness, thinking about how grief is the most private of negotiations between longing and reconciliation. It's awful what you have to give up for the sake of equilibrium, i.e., the hope that the person who has left you will somehow return. In the morning, I hit the **P** icon on my car's GPS that stands for **Parents** and I started driving. It's a seven-hour trip. Most of the way, I kept the radio off. I let my soul attend to its repair while I watched the land go by. I saw things that were so beautiful: long stretches of cirrus clouds; rolling hills; tall pines rising up out of many feet of snow, evergreen.

When I pulled into my parents' driveway, I saw that my sister and brother-in-law and parents were squeezed into the booth next to the kitchen window. Such a familiar sight, the top of my parents' heads as they sat there. I looked at what I could see of my mother's face: from where I was, she looked okay. When I came in, the smell of garlic was thick in the air: my sister had made shrimp scampi, which my mother loves. "Do you want some?" my sister asked. And I said no. I ate pasta, plain, with butter, and it was not so good because the pasta had grown cold. I used a different salad dressing than the one my sister had put out. I ate my dinner, thinking, **Why am I doing this? Why am I refusing offerings of food that I like?** And I realized it was because I was mad that Tish had died, and by God, I was going to take it out on **something**.

In the morning, I asked my mother if she would like me to bring her to her church or to the beautiful cathedral in St. Paul so that she might have some time alone. Or I would stay with her there, whatever she wanted. She said, "It may sound stupid, but you know what I would like to do? I would like to go alone to Rainbow, where we used to shop, because . . ." She began to cry, and finished, "I'll see her in the aisles." She stood there before me in her nightgown with the little red hearts, her hands clasped tightly together, and I said I understood completely why she would want to do that. We made an arrangement for her to call me when she was through. I dropped her off and went to the library to use their computers to catch up on email, and then I went to the large-print section to find something light and interesting for my mother to read. I told the librarian a little about the circumstances of my visit, and he very kindly let me check the book out on her card, and he made a note that it would be okay if it got returned late. There was a fireplace at the library, and patrons sat reading in front of it. I watched them for a while, and the sight was soothing; I hoped that after my mother moved, she might be able to take a bus here and sit before the fire herself. There was a coffee shop there and they had a lot of sweet rolls. The way my mother eats breakfast is to have coffee and a "goodie" first, the goodie being part of a sweet roll. Then, later, she'll have her real breakfast. I bought my mom a gift card at the coffee shop so she could not only check out a book from the pretty expansive large-print section, but also have a cup of coffee and a goodie. I hoped this might bring her some comfort and provide her with something to look forward to in her new life at the facility. I couldn't wait for her to get there. I was equating it with relief, with safety, with the opportunity for communion with others. But I also suspected that there was a mountain inside my mother's chest, and that dealing with the weight of it would come first for a long time.

My mother called from Rainbow just as she was ready to check out, and I drove back to the store and went inside to meet her there. She showed me the pinwheel cookies she was buying (my **expensive** cookies, she called them). After we checked out we went to the service desk to buy a betting card. My mother got one with two games on it, and she said the top game was for Tish and the bottom one was for her. Tish won nothing, but my mom won two dollars, so she went right back up to the desk to claim her fortune. And I thought, **There you go**.

On Saturday, Patty called to say that the funeral would be on Tuesday, and I was alone in the kitchen when I took that call. I expressed my condolences to Patty and she thanked me. Then she said, "I just feel so sorry for your mom." "I know," I said. "How is she doing?" Patty asked, and I thought about how my mom had lost Tish and she was losing her husband in the cruel way of dementia and her one remaining sister was having a few problems with dementia, too, and she basically had not one of her peers for support. I put my forehead in my hand and started to cry and I said, "Oh, this is just unbearable," and Patty said, "I know." But even as I said it, I knew it wasn't true. This wasn't unbearable. And besides, my mother is strong. This is something I've come to see only recently. She is much stronger than I ever gave her credit for. She will get through this with courage and grace and faith and even with a sense of humor. It will just take time, and that time will pass, as it always does, wobbly day by wobbly day.

On Sunday, I took my mother shopping for makeup and for a gift for my grandson's upcoming birthday. Then my sister came over for a while, and we made to-scale paper cutouts of our parents' furniture so that they could see how everything would fit on the floor plan they have of the apartment where they will be moving. Odd how much fun it was.

On Monday, I took my parents back to the facility to take photos of the apartment. It was completely empty now, and they could inspect the place with leisure. One of the photos I took shows my mother looking out one of the windows of the living room and she is smiling; in fact, she appears to be almost delighted. She told me she liked how deep the windowsills were; she could keep plants there. She liked how much cupboard space she would have; she liked the fact that for the first time in her life, she would have a dishwasher.

After we had finished taking photos, we sat for a while in the lobby and both my parents seemed content. I knew that coffee was always available in the dining room, so I asked my parents if they'd like a cup of coffee and they said why, yes, they would. So they drank coffee and spoke with a few of the residents, all of whom told my parents that they would love it there. "Their coffee is good, huh?" my father said, and my mother agreed that it was and so did I.

After a while, I asked my parents to come and sit in the dining room. I wanted to show them the large fireplace, before which you could sit in Queen Anne chairs; I wanted to show them how you could sit at a table by the window to eat breakfast and watch the birds come to the feeders outside, just like they did at home; I wanted to show my mother the many empty planters stacked up outside, waiting to be filled when spring came. Just as we were getting up to go, a woman approached us and said, "Oh, are you leaving?" She had a cup of coffee in her hand; she had just gotten up from a nap and had come down to find someone to talk to. She was lovely. June was her name, such a good old-fashioned name, and I thought she might be a friend for my mother.

It was a good visit; my parents both seemed pleased. When we got home, I called my sister and told her how well it had gone. Later that afternoon, I bought a huge box of See's candy for the luncheon that was going to take place after the funeral; Aunt Tish

had loved chocolate. My mother got a little box of chocolates to slip into the casket
with her sister. She put it in a cellophane bag
and added some other, loose candies and a
note: **To sustain you on your journey.** She
affixed multiple ribbons: the look was cele-
bratory. She showed it to me and said, "Do
you think that's all right?" and I said yup, I
did. Sure did.

Monday night, my mother set her alarm
so that she could wake up at six-thirty. She
wanted time to get ready for the nine-thirty
funeral, and I knew that part of getting
ready included her desire to sit alone in the
living room, in the yellow chair she always
goes to when she wakes up in the night, or
needs to put her feet up, or when she simply needs to close her eyes and tend to her
own thoughts, her own needs. She doesn't
usually get to do this for too long; my father
finds her, and often he asks, "Are you mad at
me?" He thinks if she isn't beside him, she's
mad at him. "He doesn't understand," my
mother said, when she told me about this.
I knew he didn't. But we were both a little
mad at him for not allowing my mother time
alone. I thought, **This is why I came here**

early, to shepherd my mother's grief, to make sure she has time and space to cry or reflect or simply sit in silence. But it was proving harder to do than I thought.

On the morning of the funeral, I came into the kitchen and found my mother standing there in her nightgown, looking distraught. "How are you?" I said softly, and she flung her arms up in the air, and with tears in her eyes she said, "Well, we're not moving." I asked her what she meant and she told me that once again my father had done a complete about-face. There was too much to move, it was too overwhelming. It could be too expensive. **Let's just think this over.**

"How do **you** feel?" I asked my mother. "Do you not want to go?"

"I wanted to go," she said, "but right now I just give up. Right now I'm just so confused."

"Okay," I said. "If you want to go, you'll go. You're going to have to be the decision maker. He's not able . . . It's going to be up to you. But we don't need to talk about it any more right now."

My mother told me my father was having a hard time dressing for the funeral. "His suits just hang on him," she said. She and my sister have tried to take him shopping for a new suit, but he won't go. "I told him just to wear a sweater," she told him, and I said, "Sure, that's fine, a sweater is fine."

My mother went to get dressed, and my father came into the kitchen. He was wearing a white shirt and blue pants and suspenders, and thank goodness for those suspenders. He sat at the kitchen table with me and started in about how they weren't moving. And I lost it. Between my teeth, I said, "Dad? I know this is hard, but we have talked about this and talked about this and it is just the best decision. You've said the sooner you get there, the better. You've said you know you have to go. Yesterday, you seemed to love the place." He said something to the effect of this was **their** lives and **they** would make the decision. I leaned in closer to him and said, "You are only half of this relationship. Mom wants to go. I am not going to let you bully her out of her decision. And today is **Tish's funeral**."

"Let's not argue; let's just eat our breakfast," my father said, but I had no appetite, and I doubt he did either. But we ate our breakfast. Chew, chew, chew. No eye contact. The hour before the funeral mass was the visitation, which meant the open casket was stationed in the middle of the church. There Tish was, a rosary intertwined in her hands, her fingernails painted a rose-pink color, her make-up blessedly subtle. She was wearing a turquoise blouse that my mother said she bought one day when they were out shopping, but then it went on sale so she returned it and bought it again for the sale price.

I looked at Tish's familiar face and wept, and then I looked at some pictures of her that were stationed amid the flowers and I wept more, and then I started looking through the flowers to make sure the ones I'd ordered had been sent. This felt like a tacky thing to do but I thought maybe everyone did it. I didn't like one of the bouquets I had ordered and I started to get mad, but then I realized that nothing they might have done would have been good enough.

When Tish fell, I had sent cheerful yellow bouquets to both my aunt and my mother. With my aunt's bouquet, I'd asked to have included a stuffed bear, and had also asked that the florist put something on the bear's arm so it would look like it had a broken arm, too, what with the way that misery loves company. The florist had quite cleverly fashioned a sling and a cast out of blue ribbon and Patty told me Tish had really liked that bear, and she'd had it sitting on her couch. Patty brought it to the funeral and gave it to my mom, who held on to it tightly throughout the service. Once, I saw her stroking the bear's arm with her finger, as though offering it comfort. **Hush, little baby, don't you cry.**

Patty gave a beautiful eulogy, and I have no idea how she did it. She stood up there and talked about how her mother's name came from Tish's mispronunciation of Patricia Frances: as a toddler, she called herself Tisha Pances. How she was raised as a child of the depression, how she came to marry Bob, how she was a peacemaker and wanted more than anything for her fiery, strong-willed children to get along, and how Patty hoped that in their mother's memory, they would. I cried a lot, my mother cried a little, my father put his head down in sorrow.

The lunch. The way my mother at first touched nothing on the plate I fixed for her, but then did. Cheesy scalloped potatoes were on the menu. They were delicious. The candy disappeared almost immediately so I made sure to grab three pieces for my mom and dad and . . . who? Tish, I suppose.

After the funeral, we took a drive around St. Paul so that we could go past the condo where Tish lived. It is on Grand Street, a street full of restaurants and stores and life. We went past the cathedral that Tish used to walk to—it was pretty far from her place, and as she had grown older, she had taken to finding places to sit and rest along the way. We drove past Patty's new place, which she had just signed the papers for on her mother's last day on earth. One of the reasons she had moved there was to be close to her mother, whose condo was only a block away. Tish had told my mom that if she looked out a certain window, she could see Patty's place. It was **right there**.

After we got home, my mother seemed to come fully into her sorrow. As we all stood in the kitchen, she was asked a question and she just looked so bewildered, and then she got flustered and seemed like she was ready to cry. I took her into her bedroom and sat on the bed with her and let her talk. "She was the one I would bitch to," my mother said. "And she would bitch to me." After a while, we heard my father come to stand outside the door. He said, "What are you doing in there? Locking yourself in the bedroom?" "Yes," we both said. Later, when we came out, my mother said, "I think I'll have a cup of tea, would you like a cup of tea?" Yes, I said, I would.

That night, my sister, my parents, and I went out for Mexican food. My mother, a famously poor drinker, one who gets loaded on half a glass of wine, ordered a strawberry margarita that came in a goblet big enough to float a boat. She lifted the glass and said, "To Patricia," and we all toasted. We commented on the size of the drink, and my mother said she was going to have every bit of it. "Oh boy," my father said. "Pretty soon you'll be singing 'You Are My Sunshine.'" This is something my mother has done in the past, sung when she's a little tipsy; I suppose it's her Irish blood. But she reminded my dad that she had one other song in her repertoire. She said, "I also do 'It's My Party,'" and here her face changed as she finished saying the title, "'and I'll Cry If I Want To.'" She did indeed drink the whole margarita. And then she ate all of her dinner. I couldn't believe it.

In the morning, I came downstairs and my mother was in her yellow chair. She hadn't slept well; she had been sick in the night. I remembered that when her mother, my grandmother, lost her husband, she lay on the sofa and threw up into a plastic bucket, over and over. But my mother probably got sick from drinking, and I told her that's what she got for being such a lush. She told me her ear was hurting, too, and I took a look and told her it was a little red and maybe it had gotten irritated from the way she slept on it? Probably, she said, and then she waved her hand and said, "It will go away," which is what she says about any health problem that comes along. And usually, it does go away. Not her breast cancer. That didn't go away. She had surgery for that, and I remember that when Tish came to see her she brushed my mother's hair and asked if her doctor was good-looking.

On the drive home from Minnesota, I was lost in sadness. Then my daughter Julie called, and even though you're not supposed to drive and be on the phone, I held on to that phone like it was keeping me alive. We talked about where my grandchildren should go to nursery school for a long time, and at one point Julie apologized for talking about that in the wake of all that was going on with my parents. "No, no; it's a relief to talk about this," I told her. And it was. I thought about all those little beings in nursery school classrooms bright with artwork and full of things to learn. I thought about how they were so new in life that their eyes still shone like babies' when they are born and they look up at you, trusting that all will be well.

I got home in time to go to my writers' group. It felt important to me to get back to normal as quickly as I could. It was a good session; I was glad to be in the company of those women and I was glad to take all they offered and I was glad to offer what I could to them. Being with them reminded me how I'd once heard a writer talking about meals in China, how there was always a sharing platter. On the walk home, I saw that the moon was not quite full, and that it seemed pale and insubstantial, as though it were the thinnest of wafers. But it stayed there, high up in the night sky; it followed me all the way home and it shone on after I closed my eyes and fell asleep in my own bed. My friend Marianne used to say that the best index to her mental health (after her complexion) was whether she knew what phase the moon was in. I saw what phase the moon was in, and I slept well.

On Thursday, I talked on the phone to my parents and my sister and the woman at the facility where I hoped my parents would move. Then, on Friday, I decided I would take the day off from all of this. I got my car washed and went to the cleaners and the grocery store. After I got home, I made chili and goulash and cornbread, and I roasted vegetables in olive oil and herbs de Provence. I made croutons for salad from a demi-baguette of Asiago bread. I made brownies from a recipe Julie sent me and they were the best brownies I'd ever tasted. I sent a lovely bouquet of flowers to a girlfriend for her birthday. I got some pink tulips and pussy willows and yellow mini-roses for myself.

That evening, while Bill was out working, I sat before the television and ate goulash while I watched **American Idol.** The show is a little foolish but it's fun. I like listening to people sing. I like the competitive nature of the show. I suppose it's my football. Sometimes, in the shower, I pretend I'm singing to the judges. Dressed in Eileen Fisher and emphatically flat shoes. I sing standards like "It Had to Be You" and "You're My Thrill," and in my fantasy the judges are always amused and impressed, both.

After I watched the show, I cleaned up the kitchen and thought, **Okay, now I'm going up to read Cynthia Ozick and that will be a nice ending for my day off.**

But then I couldn't stand it, and I called my parents, just to check in. My dad answered the phone and he sounded upset. "How are you?" I asked, and he said, "Not so good." When I asked him why, he said he had fallen into the bathtub and banged his head. And then he couldn't get out. "How **did** you get out?" I asked, envisioning the people who responded to the 911 call saying, **Okay, Art, put your arms around my neck.** But no. My eighty-eight-year-old mother got him out. When I talked to her, she said it had been pretty hard to tell him how to maneuver so that he could stand up again. I thought he'd been taking a shower, but she said no, he was just in the bathroom and he fell into the tub. "Good grief," I said, and she said, "It's always something. Tish and I kept saying, 'This is the winter of our discontent.' It sure is. And another major snowstorm is coming. Ah, me."

I asked if she wanted me to find out if she could move sooner than the fifteenth of March. No, she said. No, she needed to sort through some things. Mentally. She said she had called the movers who specialize in older people leaving houses they've been in for a long time. Gentle Transitions, they're called. As if. And yet I'm glad that's what they're called. I do so hope they are gentle, that they see with seeing eyes and hear with hearing ears and feel the history in that little house on the corner as something they would touch only with gloves on.

FEBRUARY 21, 2011

I remember the first time I wrote for relief. I was fifteen and worried about all kinds of things, and one day I sat at a dresser with a mirror and looked into my own eyes, searching for an answer as to who I was and what was going on inside me. No reply. So I got out a notebook and a pencil and began to write, and a heavy curtain parted.

My first novel had to do with what it was like growing up as an Army brat, calling on my memories of riding in the backseat of the car as we drove to the new place, watching the telephone poles whip past, watching too my father's eyes in the rearview mirror, always fearful that I might get in trouble for something. I also drew from things like sitting on the steps of yet another porch and waiting for kids my age to find me. Unlacing my father's combat boots for him when he came home, being afraid of those boots as well as the insignia pins on his khaki shirts. Sitting at the dinner table unmoving, my heart banging in my chest, while I or someone else got yelled at. Standing on the edge of the bathtub to look over my shoulder into the mirror at the red slap marks he'd left on my butt, as clearly outlined as if I had painted them there. The last time he hit me, it was when I was a senior in high school, and he slapped me across the face. That time, I didn't cry, and he never hit me again.

I wanted to talk about all of this, but mostly I wanted to come to peace with it. I knew other kids had had it far worse than I, whether they were Army brats or not. And I knew there were other sides to my father: all my life I had seen the love and care he directed at my mom. He had shown me things: how to thread a needle, how to dress a wound, how the Dutch Masters used light in their paintings. Whenever I saw that he approved of anything I'd done, my spirit soared. As Dory Previn's song says, **I danced to please my father, just to win one glance.**

In writing the novel, I wanted to put some memories into a mix that was largely fictionalized and see what emerged. And what emerged was compassion. Still, I worried about publishing it. I worried that I would hurt my father in ways that were unfair.

I consulted with my mother, who read the manuscript in secret, and told me that yes, I should publish it. She said, "I think it would hurt your father more if you passed up this opportunity than anything you said in the book would." When **Durable Goods** came out and my father read it, it did hurt him. But it also made him ask some questions. He asked my mother, "Was I this bad?" And she said, "Well, you were pretty bad." And then something wonderful happened: the book seemed to heal us. My dad became My Guy.

But all that's happening with my parents now: Is it unfair to publish my thoughts about it, to make it available to anyone who cares to have a look? Would I want someone writing about me losing my facilities? The answer is I don't know. But I think if it served a larger purpose, I wouldn't mind.

I brought this question to my writing group. I asked them if I should make public such intimate things about my parents. And they, all sensitive and intelligent women, said yes, I should. Because reading it helped them, when they thought about what they might be headed for with their own parents—or, ultimately, themselves. Because it would help others who were going through the same kind of experience. Because **I am he as you are he as you are me and we are all together**. But the women in my group are writers, with an innate understanding of what art demands, requires, and does. They, too, have a reflexive need to document everything that happens to them or to others close to them, one way or another. I know a writer who lost two lifelong friends when she wrote about something personal that happened to one of them. Wrote about it and published it, I should say. I didn't ask her if it was worth it. Nor did I ask her if she felt like she had no choice.

The idea of sharing such personal history is a bit like slowing down for an accident. You see people in the cars ahead of you rubbernecking, and you think they are shameful. But when you pass by the wreck, even if you don't slow down and look yourself, you want to. What compels you might be the blood and the bones, but probably not. Probably what draws you to look at an accident is the fact that it didn't happen to you. Yet. But deep in your own bones is the knowledge that it could, and so you look to imagine what it might be like. If you are a writer, you need to put what you imagine into words, and then you need to read those words in order to understand yourself. After that, you might feel a need to put those words before others. I think I have to say that **need** is the operative word.

I keep remembering what happened one time when my mother came to one of my readings, along with her sisters and a cousin who is a fan, and that cousin's husband. Many writers find it difficult to read before their families; I am certainly one of them. But there I was, standing at the lectern reading a short story that was meant to be humorous and that was told in first person. The character says that when she was in high school and would come home to find that her mother had made liver and onions for dinner, she felt like committing suicide. My mother did make liver and onions occasionally. And I hated liver then and I hate liver now and I will hate it all my life; in my mind, there is nothing you can do to liver to make it taste good. I know many people love liver. I know many people love tongue. I know many people love rides at the state fair that make me throw up. If you catch my drift. But I plucked that real-life detail of hating liver to put in a fictional story to serve a larger purpose, having to do with the complex relationship between women and food. When I had finished reading the story, my cousin's husband's hand shot up. Eyes blazing, he asked, "What did your mother cook that you **did** like?"

"Um. This is **fiction**," I might have said, but I answered by listing some things my mother made that were sensational: Enchiladas. Goulash. Apple crisp. I think I might also have confessed that I used to lie by the stove just to smell certain things baking. Thus

I admitted culpability for a crime I never intended but that clearly he thought I'd committed.

I see his eyes now, I still see his eyes: accusing. Appraising me as a selfish show-off, an ungrateful bitch, a bottom-feeding opportunist. He was only one person in that audience, but when I think back on that reading, oftentimes he is all I see. But. Recalling his contempt for me on that day makes me decide on this day what to do.

FEBRUARY 23, 2011

In the basement, my neighbor Bob, who is the contractor who rehabbed my house, is working on fixing my furnace. He tells me he's just back from Oxford, Mississippi, where he watched his star-in-the-making son play baseball. He asks if I've ever been to Oxford, and I say yes, indeed; I love Oxford; I love the **South**.

Bob says he loved it, too; that the people were just so nice. And the town square was cool. And college kids were drinking all over the place. He tells me Essie was a big hit, referring to the family's bulldog, whose formal name is Esther, and if that isn't the perfect name for a bulldog who resembles nothing so much as a fireplug, I don't know what is.

Bob asks how I'm doing and I tell him I'm going through a lot of stuff having to do with my parents right now. I fill him in and then tell him some happy news:

Last night I called my parents and learned that they had liked Gentle Transitions. My mother said the woman who came out was thorough and patient and not pushy and that they are going to hire the company to pack what they wanted to keep, move it, and then unpack everything. Dust off your hands, put your fists to your hips, voilà. She told me the amount the company would charge, which she thought was staggering, but which I thought was a good deal, and I told her so. I said, "Go ahead and let them do it all; on moving day, I'll come up and we'll all go out and play." And she laughed. She made mention of some things she would miss: her garden, the nearby park.

"Right," I said. "I haven't been through this, so I don't know exactly how you feel. I do know it must be so hard. But there is a garden at the place you're going to, and there's a little trail you can walk on by the stream. Mostly, I think that there is still joy to be had for you two, and that you will find some there. In any case, it will be a lot easier for you both."

Next I talked to my dad, and he said, "Well, we decided to go ahead and just let them do it. It costs a lot, but we can afford it." He seemed like his old self, in charge of his life, completely aware of what was going on and in support of it. I was going to offer to pay for the move, but I realized it would take something away from him if I did. He has talked about feeling emasculated because he believes he is no longer taking care of his wife. Well, now he is. Now, together, they are moving forward.

This morning, I got an email from Vicki with my parents' budget information. She listed their income, which is modest, and their expenses, also relatively modest. I thought, **Well, this will be helpful**, and started looking at the spreadsheet. My sister is a very thorough person, and in the expenses, she had listed all the magazines my parents subscribe to, even though both of them have trouble seeing now. They get **Country Living, Birds & Blooms, Family Circle, Good Housekeeping, Ladies' Home Journal, Looking Back, National Geographic,**

National Geographic Traveler, Reader's Digest, Smithsonian, Woman's Day, and **Taste of Home.**

I read this list of publications and it seemed so innocent to me, so dear. I thought about how you can tell a lot about a person by looking at what magazines they subscribe to. I thought about how I was raised with magazines fanned out on a coffee table next to the sweet potato plant, various women's magazines and **Life** and **The Saturday Evening Post** with the Norman Rockwell covers. I thought about how, for years, I followed my mother's lead and bought **Family Circle** and **Woman's Day** at the grocery store, and tore recipes out of them with abandon; I found some really good recipes in them that I still use today. I thought of how I used to sit next to my sister on the sofa, watching her read magazines; how she turned the pages in a very specific and deliberate way. First, she delicately licked her finger. Then she turned the page from the very edge of the bottom right-hand corner, and she turned it slowly. She made reading a magazine look like paper ballet. Whenever I tried to read a magazine like her, it just wasn't the same. It wasn't a cool ritual practiced by a glamorous teenager with bobby socks and loafers and jeans rolled to the knee; it was just me, a flat-chested poseur with crooked bangs, turning the pages all wrong and in any case not finding what was on those pages nearly as alluring as when I was looking over my sister's shoulder.

Next on the spreadsheet, I consulted the charitable donations column, and was dumbstruck. My parents, with their modest income, give to: Alzheimer's Foundation. American Institute for Cancer Research. National Foundation for Cancer Research. American Heart. American Lung. American Veterans. Boys Town. Holy Childhood Church. Friends of Como Park. Doctors Without Borders. Easterseals. Friends of the Library. Smile Train. Special Olympics. St. B's Indian School. Gillette Children's Specialty Hospital. Minnesota Hospice. Humane Society. Listening House. Little Sisters of the Poor. March of Dimes. Maryknoll Sisters. Mercy Home. Paralyzed Vets. Salvation Army. VFW.

I read that long list and then I read it again. And then I looked out the window and saw not one single thing except this:

I can live a long life and for every day of that long life make mighty efforts to improve myself, but I will never be as decent a person as either of my parents is. Not even close.

Bob told me his dad had moved to a place for retirees, and that at first he had hated it. "But, you know," Bob said, "before he moved there, I used to call him just to check on him—I was really worried about him living alone. I'd call and say, 'Hey, Dad, what are you doing?' and he would say, 'Nothing. I'm just sitting here. Having a martini before I go to bed.' I'd say, 'Dad, it's **six o'clock**,' and he'd say, 'Yeah, well, I get up at four.' But now he's not there half the time. He's out having dinner with friends, or a bunch of them went out somewhere together. Your parents will love it."

"I know," I said, and I did not tell him that when I spoke to my sister about selling the house in the spring when my mother's tulips would be coming up, I sobbed. But you know? Happily.

MARCH 6, 2011

When my younger daughter was five years old, she went one day with a friend and that friend's mother to a play-ground. She was delivered home soon afterward by the friend's apologetic mother, who said that Jenny had fallen off the jungle gym and hurt her arm. I'll say. It was broken in two places.

Jenny didn't cry, at first. She walked all the way home, holding her pain and tears at bay for the fifteen or so minutes that it took to get there, but as soon as she was released to my custody and I shut the front door, she let loose, howling with pain. I flung off my apron, told my older daughter to sit with Jenny in the backseat of the car, and drove to the emergency room. Jenny was X-rayed, casted, and put into a sling, and that night she came home and was read books before bed, as usual.

The next morning, I had a moment of worry about the best way for me to take a shower, because I didn't want to get my cast wet. Then I remembered I wasn't the one with the cast. I was just overidentifying with someone I loved, trying to take her broken arm for her.

Something similar is happening now, with my parents. Last week I dreamed about being a much older woman, a mass of shock-white untamable hair around my head, a bowed torso, big brown age spots on my legs, worry in my mind and my heart and my soul about how I am going to fare after I leave a place so familiar to me, so dear and so full of memories. Last night I dreamed I was living in the apartment my parents are going to, and I was knocking on all the doors of the people who lived down the hall, wanting to see who they were.

Things are getting harder at my parents' house. My mother has come into some anger, which is always a good catchall for feelings of grief, of fear, of pain, of longing, of regret.

My father is confused. He takes her anger personally, as it is sometimes intended, and he doesn't know what he has done wrong. He can't remember that he has asked the same question many times over. When he asks questions of the people who have been asked to come to the house, when he asks what (the hell) they are doing there, he is trying to protect her, not humiliate her. The other day, he asked if she was embarrassed to walk with him, because she is always rushing ahead. She has told my sister she thinks he could stop that shuffling gait if he wanted to.

Ah, me.

Nothing for it but to plan a party, say I. (A friend of mine, once hearing me come out with some wildly optimistic outburst, laughed, leaned into my face, and imitating Pollyanna, said, "I'm **glad** my legs are broken; glad, glad, glad!")

Never mind. I'm planning a surprise housewarming party for the Saturday after my parents have moved in to the new place. I'll call a really good bakery and order the biggest sheet cake they make for what will surely be a smallish gathering, but my plan is that the leftovers will be shared with the new neighbors and the staff. My mother has been talking about all the memories in the house they're leaving behind, and so here I come like a locomotive down the tracks: **Don't worry! We'll start making** new **memories right away!**

This morning, I awakened wondering if my mother will be mad at me for doing this, and if my father will be confused by it. I hope not.

In a solicitation by a realtor that came to my house in the mail the other day was a seed packet. Forget-me-nots. I had been planning on buying my mother a new and beautiful gardening tool, to remind her that she can still spend time digging in the dirt, inhaling the scent of both it and the blossoms she so adores. Now I think I'll throw in that packet of seeds, too.

I hope she'll plant forget-me-nots in the woods she looks out onto, and that every time she sees them she will think she is making the most of her situation. I hope she'll think of her life as having been well lived and, on balance, lucky. I hope she'll go down to the community breakfasts and make new friends. I hope she'll start a book club and ride the bus to go shopping for birthday presents for her great-grandchildren. I hope my father will find some vets and sit in the corner of the dining room drinking coffee with them and talking about their glory days, and that he will go out to breakfasts with them to a place where the waitresses are bodacious and flirtatious. I hope my mother will look in the refrigerator one day and see that they're out of milk and tell my dad to hop on his mobility scooter and go to the store at the end of their hall to get more. I hope my parents will go out to dinner on a double date, even if it's no farther than the dining room one floor down from their apartment. I am, as is easy to see, full of hope. But I have to remember something I always forget: you can't tell anyone else how to experience something. People live behind their own eyes. I'm not the one with the broken arm.

MARCH 23, 2011

It is done. My parents are living at a place that has Eagle in its name, even though mostly what you see when you look out their windows are crows. But you also see the loveliness of the woods and the meandering stream, where ducks take off and land in spectacular ways, like little boys showing off for each other. You see the sky. The light comes in. At night, there is the moon, visible through the branches of the trees.

I went up to Minnesota in advance of the move and spent the last few days in my parents' house with them. One night, I lay in the attic bedroom and thought about how, really, this house should not mean much to me. I lived there only one summer. And then I thought about how I had brought my daughters there from the time they were babies, and how, in this bedroom where they slept on a cot across from me, they used to like to look at the lit-up Christmas decorations on the wall. I thought of how, on the kitchen table, my dad rolled strudel dough out so thin you could read newsprint through it, and how he stirred homemade lentil soup on the stove, and how, when his wife and his sisters-in-law were out shopping, he bustled in the kitchen so as to have dinner ready for them when they came back. And then I began to cry, but it was a removed and abstract kind of crying, a punch-the-time-clock type of grief. Mostly, I wanted to get my parents out of a place that had become a kind of hell to them. You don't eat breakfast in the past, the smell of apple strudel in the air. You sit at the table with the situation as it is, and the situation was that my mother was about to murder my dad, and my dad's world had shrunk so badly he barely moved at all. It seemed to me that his lack of interaction with others was making him run around in his own brain like a hamster. It seemed he was infecting himself with paranoia and nursing his delusions as though that were the only hobby left to him. But that is only how it seemed. The truth is, he couldn't help it. Once, I drove him to get a haircut and he said, in a heartbreakingly bewildered way, "I just feel like I'm in a **fog**."

Among the things we did before the move was to attend a St. Patrick's Day dinner. Tish's daughter, Patty, hosted it, and she is a terrific cook. There was corned beef and cabbage, and carrots, and parsley buttered potatoes, and a beautifully rustic soda bread, and a pear tart for dessert. Mostly, though, there was a small group of older people, a stark reminder that there are so few from that big crowd that used to gather together for donuts and coffee. My parents and Aunt Lala, who still calls me Bethie—that's who's left of the six sisters and one brother (and their spouses) that were my mother's family. On the ride back to her house, my mother asked Lala what she had done that day. "Well, I dusted the living room and the bedroom," she said. Such a small circle our lives can get put into. I wish Lala would move, too.

In advance of the move, my parents and I went to their new home to take care of a few things, and while we were there, we attended the weekly ice-cream social. We sat with Lucille, the woman who is going to be my parents' next-door neighbor. She is a warm and friendly woman, feisty, too. She wrote to the president of the company that runs the complex to complain about the television service being screwed up. She was steamed because she wasn't getting sports and she wanted to watch baseball and football and the hockey games, too. "Everybody was complaining about the television service, but no one was doing anything about it," she said. "So I wrote the president—just mailed the letter yesterday." She widened her eyes and covered her mouth and I said, "Good for you." Lucille is the one responsible for getting tickets to the symphony: if you want to ride the bus to go and hear music, why, just let Lucille know, and she'll sign you up.

When we drove home from the place that day, my dad was very quiet in the backseat. Then he said, "Well, the bill at Herberger's is going to go up. I'm going to have to get some new clothes. Those people dress to the nines!"

I told my friend Wanda about this— her ninety-five-year-old parents live at the complex, too; in fact, she's the one who told me about it. When I met Wanda, I was twenty-three and involved with the guy who lived downstairs from her. She and I were young and a little wild and we rode on the back of our boyfriends' motorcycles, and when Wanda laughed, she laughed really long and **loudly**. She had long blond hair and I had long black hair and I think it's safe to say we both thought we were hot stuff. We've kept in touch intermittently over the years, and now here we are meeting again at this place where the old people live. "Who would have predicted **this**?" Wanda said.

Anyway, when I told Wanda what my father said about people dressing to the nines, she laughed and laughed, and I was happy to see she still laughed long and hard. Then she said, "You know, I was going out shopping for my parents the other day and I said, 'Okay, you two. I'm going out for diapers for both of you. Do you need anything else?' My dad said, 'See these black suspenders? I could use some khaki ones.' So I went right over to Kohl's and I got him some khaki suspenders." I know how she felt, doing that. There is something about doing such things for aging parents who can't do for themselves any longer; there is a unique sorrow but satisfaction in it. I suppose there's some real exhaustion in it, too, but I live far enough away that I don't feel that. I don't run errands for my parents all that often.

After Wanda told me about getting the suspenders, she got quiet. Then she said, "You know what? We both of us should buy stock in whatever company makes Depends. Seriously. We should buy stock in Depends."

On the day of the move, I took my dad over to the new place right after the movers came. The house he was leaving was crowded and chaotic: no country for old men, so to speak. The new place was empty but for the birds we'd brought over the day before. Their cage was on a TV tray, positioned before a window. I'd brought along a folding chair for my dad to sit on; I set it up right next to the birds. Before he sat down, though, before he even took off his coat, he stood before his beloved budgies, his hat in his hand, and he leaned forward and spoke gently to them. "Do you think you're going to like it here?" he asked. "Do you? . . . Frieda? . . . Fritzi?" Then my dad took off his coat and sat down and began his wait, displaying a patience he was never capable of before.

When my mother arrived she was enraged, which is to say that her heart was breaking because her house was being taken from her, which is to say that her life was. She was not thinking that she is an eighty-eight-year-old woman whose circumstances will be made better by this move; she was grieving the fact that she is no longer in her forties and standing on the sidewalk outside the house her husband just bought her and admiring the bay window. She was incensed that her sister Tish was no longer there. She sat defiantly silent, scowling, as the movers brought things into the apartment, and when we asked her if she'd like to go for lunch, she said nothing. When we asked again, she said, in a kind of muted, vicious way, "I don't care. I'm not hungry." And I glared at her. I glared at her and got pissed off at her and thought, **What do you** want? **You said you wanted to move here! We all worked so hard to get you here, and now you don't want to be here?**

I know that was wrong. Cruel and unfeeling. I know such a reaction betrays everything

I have learned about the human heart and suffering and defense and the various disguises of pain and the need for patience. But I wanted to reach over and slap her and say **Stop it!**

The new apartment came together beautifully, and by Saturday, when we had the party, my parents both seemed in high spirits. We invited not only relatives, but a couple who live down the hall, Kay and Bit, my dad sat happily kibitzing with Bit the whole time. My dad was a lifer in the Army; Bit was a major general in the Air Force, so you can just imagine. At one point my brother, who came from Hawaii to do his part in the move, showed a bunch of old military magazines from World War II to Bit, but he barely looked: they were Navy.

On the day I left to go home, Vicki was at my parents' new place, and she asked our dad to come with her to the exercise room, right down the hall, so that she could show him how to work a machine he might use. Nah, he said, he didn't want to. Earlier, I had asked him about taking a walk with me and he said, Nah, he didn't want to. So when I heard him refuse Vicki, too, I said, "Hey,

Dad. You know how you keep saying you can't thank us enough for our help, financial and physical, you just can't thank us enough, blah blah blah? Well, here's what you can do to thank us: you can take care of yourself, and part of taking care of yourself means getting a little exercise and trying to build up your strength and being able to walk a bit. Come to the exercise room with us! Let Vicki just show you something! Spend five minutes there, that's all! **Try!**"

Both my parents dutifully followed my sister and me to the exercise room and we put my mom on a bike type thing and my dad on something that would work his legs, and we gave them a three-minute workout, and when we left, we were all smiling. I don't think it's exaggerating to say that my parents had a bit of fun. That seemed very clear to me.

But when it was time for Vicki to take me to the airport, and we said goodbye, I closed the front door of the apartment and I looked at Vicki and put my finger to my lips. Then I stood in the hall with my ear close to the door. I heard my dad say, "You know, I love them, but sometimes they drive me **nuts**!" He must have looked at my mother for agreement then, saying, "Huh?" and I heard her say a tentative "... **Ja** ..." I told Vicki what I'd heard and she laughed and said, "Yeah, well, right back at you." I was happy. I thought, **Good! Be allied against us. Be** allied. **And be energized, even if it's only in anger.**

❁

Tuesday night, my father accompanied my mother to the basement of the complex, to the recycling room. He had wanted to ride his mobility scooter, but my mother made him walk. In the basement, he tripped over something and fell. At first, he seemed okay—just a skinned elbow, my mother said, which she said she fixed up. Later that night, though, he asked her to call the paramedics—he thought he was going to die. He was admitted to the hospital and diagnosed with pneumonia and there are some concerns about his heart, too. He'll be okay, but he may need to stay in the hospital for a couple of days.

Naturally, I am guilty. **Walk!** Vicki and I said. **Exercise!** So he walked, and look what happened. I'm thinking of changing my tactics and saying: **Stay in a chair with a blanket over your knees! Don't get up!** But the truth is, he fell in part because he's not used to walking. He did so little in the old place, he got weak. He can get better.

So for the time being, he lies in a hospital bed and he is very worried about my mother. His nurse told me he kept saying he had to get home and make sure she was all right. I called my mother that afternoon and told her to call him and reassure him that she was fine. "You **are** fine, aren't you?" I asked. "I mean, at least you have people around you now."

"Oh, I'm just putzing around here," she said. Kay had called to check on her. Lucille had called. My mother asked me what time it was. I told her two-thirty. Okay, she said. She would call my dad and talk to him, and then go down to see if she could catch the end of the ice-cream social—she knew Lucille was going.

The first night my parents moved into the apartment, my dad asked my mother, "Does this hotel change the towels?" Also he asked her, "Isn't it nice to be here and not have those people sneaking around?" But that's all he's said that would indicate any paranoia or confusion. I know he has dementia, but I have seen that he does better when he's around people, and I think he will improve, living there. He told someone at the party that he loved it there. I hope he hurries home from the hospital.

Here the sky is gray again, but the flowers of spring are defiantly here. The buds are swelling. The great cycle of life presses on, whether we are ready or not. There is a quote I read today, something author Louis Adamic's grandfather said: life is like licking honey off a thorn. Well, yes. And what a thorn. But, oh, what honey.

My mother hates the new place. When I called to ask how it was going, I hardly recognized her voice. **"Mom?"** I said, and she said, **"What."**

"Are you . . . What are you doing?" I asked.

"Unloading the dishwasher," she said, in a way that sounded like she was saying, "So **yooou** thought a dishwasher would be **swell.** You thought I'd just **loooove** having a **dishwasher.**"

One can't leave a telephone conversation the way one backs out of a room where one senses one isn't welcome. So I plunged in and said, "Not so crazy about the place, huh?" And she said, "Not so crazy about living anymore."

"Ah," I said. And when I asked her for specifics, she answered in the dull and vague way of the depressive: **What difference does it make what I say? I am drowning forever.**

I spoke to my father, and he told me he liked it there, that he hadn't met anyone he didn't like.

I thought, **It's a good thing I'm going to be there on book tour in a few days**. I also thought, **Oh God, what now**?

When I arrived in Minnesota, I went to see my parents between a television interview I did that morning and a reading I would be doing that night. When I came into the apartment, my mother made no move toward me; she did not smile. I sat with her at the little table in the kitchen and we chatted a bit about the television interview, which she had watched. I offered her the many books I'd bought for her, providing a tempting synopsis of each, like a publishing house sales rep. My father wandered in and he embraced me and asked how I was and I said I was fine, I was fine; how was he? "I'm okay," he said, and he did indeed seem to be. Every time I hear my father say he is okay it's like seeing a flag get hoisted to the top of the pole, where it snaps in the wind.

I had brought some cookies, and I asked my parents if they wanted some. Yes, they did. "Milk?" I asked, and my mother said yes. I went to the cupboard to get a glass to pour her some and saw some dishes out on the counter. "Do you want me to put these away?" I asked, and she waved her hand in annoyance and said something about not being sure where they went, that she needed to reorganize the cupboard again, things still weren't in the right place. I surveyed the shelf where she had glasses and said, "These shelves are pretty high for you, huh?" and she said angrily that she didn't know why they built shelves so high in housing for seniors. "We can get you one of those plastic things with two steps," I said. "Lightweight, so it's easy to move around, rather than your step stool."

"Not so fast," she said, "I may be moving back to the house."

"Still thinking about that?" I asked, and she said yes and then began going through expenses, saying that for the amount of money she was paying there, if she moved back, she could hire someone to cut the grass, shovel the snow. "I lie awake at night thinking about all this," she said.

But what about transportation? I wanted to say. **The lack of interaction with people? The difficulty you had with the stairs going to the basement? Navigating the outdoor stairs in the winter?** But I had no time to get into it. I had to go and do a reading. I left my mild-eyed father and my enraged mother and I had an awful feeling going out the door, like I was leaving a child in the care of someone who had made no secret of the fact that she didn't like children.

Early the next morning, my sister and I were going to accompany my parents to the VA hospital, where my father's cognitive skills would be assessed in a more thorough way than they had been before. Before, he had been told that he had a mild cognitive disorder. But, "He's worse," my mother had mouthed to me when I arrived for this visit, and she had intimated the same on the phone before I arrived. There seemed to be grim pleasure for her in thinking that her suspicions would be validated. She seemed to want him to be diagnosed with Alzheimer's. Indeed, on the first day they moved into the apartment, my mother had asked me with ill-disguised eagerness, "So do you think the next step is to get the diagnosis of Alzheimer's?" I suspected that she thought she could then have him put away. I said that, then asked, "And what do you think you'd do then? Where do you think **you'd** live?"

"Oh," she said. "I guess I couldn't stay here, huh?"

I said icily, "No, you couldn't stay here. You couldn't afford it." The truth is that she could afford it, because I would help her. She knows that. But I wanted to take it away from her, even if I was only pretending to take it away from her. I wanted to take it away from her because she was being cruel to my dad in so many ways—wanting to push his diagnosis, pretending not to hear him when he spoke to her, refusing to go down to the dining room to have dinner with him when he suggested it—and he doesn't know why. How strange the world must seem to him now, how wavering and unreal. Like living underwater.

When I was there, my father asked, almost

shyly, almost as if it were a first date, if my mother would like to go down to dinner with him that night. And she chastised him, saying that they would have had to have signed up by eleven, you couldn't just go to dinner, you had to sign **up**! To me, sitting there listening, the tone of her voice implied three things: their dinners are stupid and the rule for signing up is stupid, and he is stupid for forgetting about the rule. I suggested that there may be room, anyway, for two more, that two more people is not so much. "Would you like me to call and see?" I asked, and my mother stared past me. "No," she said. "No."

"Do you have a menu so that you can see if you would like to make reservations for another night?"

"No," she said. "Uh-uh."

Menus are readily available just outside the front office—a big stack of them are kept in a wooden holder. There is also a board where the menu for the day is posted, stationed right beside the sign-up sheet near the dining room. Also the menus are in a weekly flyer that gets delivered to each apartment. But "No," my mother said. "Uh-uh." Which I think might have been her way of saying,

"You want to know what you know, Elizabeth Ann Berg? Nothing. That's what you know."

I looked at my dad. He shrugged. He forgets that he forgets; he doesn't know why the woman he still adores has turned on him so. I know my mother has suffered mightily. I know she's had enough, that she is sad and frustrated and still grieving her sister. But I will not be in cahoots with her in pushing my dad to be more compromised than he is. He is still himself. Failing in slow motion, yes. But he is still himself. And he is my dad, my imperfect hero, then, now, always.

Still, later that night, I lay in bed and tried to see things from my mother's point of view. She is trapped again, in an unfamiliar place that in her words "does not feel like home." And she's right: it doesn't feel like home. It isn't home. Her home is the white house on the corner with impatiens in the window boxes, the house she lived in for forty-five years, with the pantry in the basement and the dining room where so many dinners were held, so many parties given. The house where her sisters and she sat around the kitchen table or on the patio outside, smoking and talking; the place where, at Christmas, even the bathroom was decorated. She wants to go back to her house and she can't. It sits empty, and I think all of us in the family anthropo- morphize, thinking the house weeps, too.

And her husband, the man she depended on for so many years. For so **many**. The man she combed her hair for and put on lipstick for every night before he came home for so many years. He is so mightily compromised now. She must make the decisions, balance the checkbook, cook, clean, remind him to take his medication, remind him of practi- cally everything. If she goes out without him, she worries about him. Has he fallen? Has he come out into the hall looking for her? At night, she must suffer through his rest- lessness, his talking out loud. It's as though someone wheeled a shiny new ten-speed to her door and said, "Hey, you eighty-eight- year-old woman who never learned to ride a bike! How about hopping up on **this** one?" And it is not an invitation. It is a directive. There she sits, high up on an uncomfortable seat, leaning toward the handlebars, disori- ented, frightened, ill-prepared and without choice: she must pedal forward into what- ever is ahead. It comes to me that when she says she is "waiting for the other shoe to drop," she means that the landscape she is riding through is ever shifting, ever worsening. Surely some end will soon be reached, one way or another, and whatever it is, it will be fearsome and ugly.

And there is this: my father has left her before he has left her. What is a woman to do with this? Fall to her knees and weep? She would be justified in doing so. Square her chin and toughen up while at the same time offering limitless compassion? That would be nice, but it's impossible. She finds herself living in anger and despair. Hating the man she loves. And we don't help, we children, with the way we side with one of them, then the other; and now it is his turn to have us on his side, and we are vilifying her because when we have someone to blame, all of this is less painful for us. In a way, she is taking care of us more than she ever did before, at the same time that she is taking care of him. Or trying to. However much we may condemn her, she is trying to take care of him. She has to. On Monday and Tuesday and Wednesday. At nine o'clock, ten o'clock, eleven. Right now, all the time, she has to.

In the morning, my parents, my sister, and I went to the VA Hospital, a vast institution with a maze of hallways and signs everywhere to help people find where they need to go. It was another gray and rainy day, cold out, no comfort there. My father had two appointments: first, he needed to be evaluated mentally; then he needed to be fitted with a walker, which my mother found disgusting. More than once, she has said that my father's difficulty in ambulation has to do with his lack of will: he doesn't need to drag his feet that way. She walks ahead of him to convey her displeasure at what she sees as his deliberate lack of cooperation.

We were all put into a room, and when the doctor came in, he explained that he would be doing some more in-depth testing on my dad, and that he would also like to hear from each of us. He asked my mother a series of questions about my father: how long it had been since she had noticed changes in his mentation, how they manifested, had my father's delusions ever included him, say, talking to the people he "saw" when they were back in the old place. "No," she said, he never talked back to them. Did he ever have to be reminded to take care of himself—to keep himself cleaned and groomed? My mother shook her head and looked at her lap and said, "No." And when she denied that he needed help with these things, I felt that for one moment, at least, she had moved back to his side.

I thought of the Old Spice my father always used to wear, the way he would not come into the kitchen until he was shaved and his hair combed. He might still be in his bathrobe, but the lapels would be lying flat, and he would be groomed. He would, in fact, be better groomed than his wife and his younger daughter (me), we two women who did not bother to comb our hair or wash our faces before plunking down at the kitchen table for that first delicious cup of coffee.

The doctor asked about how well my father walked and my mother said disdainfully, "I'd say it was more of a **shuffle**." And I wanted to reach behind my father's back to where she sat on his other side and pinch her.

When it was my sister's turn to talk, she

mentioned that my dad had gotten signifi-
cantly weaker. That his other doctor had
said his heart murmur now sounded like a
snowblower. The doctor looked for confir-
mation of this in the chart and noted that
my father's congestive heart failure and aortic
valve stenosis were new. Yes, my sister said,
those were new. And when she said this, it
was as though she made a blanket of the air,
and drew herself into it for comfort. The way
she spoke was both gentle and defensive. She
told the doctor she thought my father had
begun to change after he developed macular degeneration and hearing loss. His world
got a lot smaller when he couldn't read the
paper or hear the news or drive anywhere
anymore. Implicit in this was: **What do you
think would happen to** you **if you were so
deprived?**

When it was my turn, I said that my concern was that my father get the best care
possible and that we find a way to give my
mother the support she needs, physical and
mental.

All this time, in the midst of us, my father
sat in his wheelchair, erect and as dignified
as he could be. His hat was on his head with

the bill centered exactly in the middle of his forehead; his hands were folded in his lap. All of us blabbing about him and him not saying one word to clarify or to defend himself in any way. If I had been my dad and my wife had said I shuffled, in that arch way, I'd have given her a look, at least. He did not react defensively to anything anyone said. He sat still, letting us talk.

Then it was his turn. The doctor asked him if he was having any trouble with his memory. "Yeah, I am," my dad said, but he did not quantify or qualify; he just told the truth, which he always does. He will not lie. Ever. "Is your memory loss causing any problems?" the doctor asked, and my dad said yes, it was causing a lot of arguments between him and his wife.

The doctor asked him if he knew the date. A moment, and then my father gave the correct day. The month? He got it right. The season? "It's supposed to be spring," my dad said, and I hoped the doctor would understand that my dad was referring to the fact that it had actually snowed last night. How about the year? the doctor asked, and my dad hesitated, then chuckled. "Haven't thought about that for a while," he said, and the doctor sat still, waiting. Finally, "Eleven," my dad said. "Two thousand eleven," and I actually felt my heart jump up in joy.

"Do you read the paper or listen to the news?" the doctor asked, and my dad said sometimes. "There's been a lot in the news lately about Japan," the doctor said, referring to the earthquake and tsunami. "Do you know what's going on in Japan?"

"Well, I believe they got some water there," my dad said.

"Any injuries?" the doctor asked.

"I assume so," my dad said.

"What caused the water problem?" the doctor asked, and my dad said he didn't know.

"What's going on in Libya?" the doctor asked, and my father said, "I don't know."

I thought, **Didn't you just hear what my sister said? Our dad can't hear well—he doesn't hear the news.** And I didn't believe he and my mother talked about the news. I thought, **I'll bet if you asked "normal" people what was going on in Libya, a large percentage of them wouldn't be able to answer.** Sad but true.

The doctor said he was going to give my

dad some tests now, okay? Okay, my dad said, most agreeably, but I felt my guard go up. The doctor said, "I'm going to give you three words, and I want you to try to remember them. The words are: **village, heaven,** and **finger**." He repeated the words, then asked my dad to say them back, which he did. They talked a bit more and then the doctor said, "What were the three words?" My dad sat still. Finally, the doctor said, "One of the words started with an **f**, like Frank." Silence. Finally, my dad shrugged and offered the doctor his upturned palms. "Lost it," he said.

"Was it **friendly, finger**, or **frankfurter**?" the doctor asked, and my dad said immediately, "Finger!" This happened many times. Just that way. My dad never remembered until it was multiple choice. But he did remember then.

My father was asked to count backward from one hundred by sevens, and he did very well. Better than my sister or my mother or I could have.

He asked my dad to draw a clock. My dad can hardly see to write, but I watched him make a rather small circle. He wrote in the twelve, three, six, and nine, and then squeezed in the other numbers. It was hard for him to do; the circle he drew was small, his vision is so compromised, and it's not easy to draw and write when a paper is being held up before you. "Now make the clock read 11:10," the doctor said, and my dad did that more or less correctly—it was hard to do because the numbers were smashed together a bit. But he did it. And the doctor did not say, "Very good." But I did, inside.

The doctor took my dad out in the hall to check his balance and to watch him walk. He brought him back in and sat him down and asked him to look up and down, left and right. He looked in my dad's mouth. He tested his peripheral vision.

When the doctor had finished testing, he sat back in his chair and said to my dad, "I understand that what you were diagnosed with before was mild cognitive disorder. But I would say you have early Alzheimer's disease. It's all semantics, really, but I would say you have that."

I thought two things right away. One was **Don't you say that about my dad.** The other was **Oh my God, how will my mother manage this?** My sister was sitting next to me, and later I learned that the two things she was feeling were this: **Well, I hope Mom's happy now. She got her diagnosis.** The other was **So what? His heart disease will kill him before his Alzheimer's will.** Mostly, though, like me, she got a new layer of ache inside.

Any questions before you leave? the doctor asked. He had told us that my dad would have to come back again, and that we would need a family conference to best decide how to care for my parents. He had said in unequivocal terms that my mother could not live in their old house anymore—not with my dad, not without him. So there went my mother's escape hatch.

I didn't like this doctor very much. I didn't think he was the most compassionate of men. I didn't see any signs that he had much of a sense of humor. He didn't seem particularly sensitive to the fact that my father was embarrassed by his failings, and that he had been subjected to difficult testing in front of an audience, not only of family members, but also a doctor in training, who sat on a little stool at the back and seemed to have trouble staying interested in what was

going on before him. **Late night last night?**
I wanted to ask him.

Did we have any questions? the doctor
wanted to know. I did have some questions.
They were:

How about I test you, buster? Can you
make chicken paprikash without a recipe
and speak German fluently? Could you have
fought in two wars? Could you bury an eight-
month-old daughter? Can you sew a straight
seam by hand and whistle like a bird and sing
ba-ba-ba-boo like Bing Crosby? Could you
have gone back to school as an adult and ex-
celled in trigonometry? Are you able to be
nonjudgmental? Could you stay married to
the same woman for sixty-eight years?

"No," I said. "No questions."

Later that night, I attended a dinner and
did a reading for a fundraiser, and I brought
my mother and sister along with me. My
nephew, Jeff, stayed with my father. After
the reading, I went up to the apartment with
my mother and sat chatting with her and my
father. I felt a kind of desperation: I was leaving the next morning, this would be the last
time I saw them for a while, and there were
things I felt needed to be resolved. I made

my way into the question of how it was going there, **really.** Again, my father said he liked it there. Again, my mother talked about how there were too many old people. Oh, she knew she was old herself, she said, but she didn't want to be around all those other old people. My father laughed and said, Well, he did. He liked being around people his own age; he didn't want to be around "teenagers, with their rock and roll." He said, "This is my idea of retirement, just relaxing a little."

"Well, that's where I disagree with you," my mother said. "I think if you just sit around all the time, you get old."

I told my mother that from my vantage point, she didn't really seem to be trying. If she wanted to see other people, she could go to the church that the bus will take her to, to the mall that is close by. Young children play on the playground attached to her building, and if she wanted to, she could volunteer to read to the kids. There is a college campus across the street she can walk to, where concerts are given that she could attend if she felt like it. She could go to the public library and wander the stacks, and then treat herself to a scone and tea.

I told her that she seemed full of criticism, full of complaint. "When your new neighbors moved in and I asked you about them, all you told me is that she was on a walker and he used a cane. What about the **people** behind the walker and the cane? What bothers you so much about seeing a walker or a wheelchair?"

"Well," she said, "to be honest, I might be in one myself one day. Why do I have to see it before it happens?"

"But if you get to know people using such things, their equipment disappears. You concentrate on the personality, not the assistive device."

She shrugged.

"You seem so angry all the time," I told her. "But you're the one who wanted to come here!"

"I didn't realize it would be like this," she said. "It's like a morgue around here."

"But you still have a lot you're interested in," I said. "You have a lot of joy inside."

"Not anymore," she said, bitterly.

So much was taken from my mother when her sister died, and she still has not had time to properly grieve her. But now I said, "What if you had died and Tish had lived? She would have mourned you, but she would have gone on with her life. She would have stayed involved in her children's and her grandchildren's lives. She would have been giving dinners for people all the time; she was a very giving person."

My mother raised her chin. "So what you're saying is that I'm not a giving person."

I hesitated, then said, "I think you could be a little more giving."

Silence.

"I know it's been hard," I said. "I know it's not perfect here. But like the doctor suggested today, it's safe here—you really couldn't stay in the house. And I think you need to try some things, to just . . . Have you tried the book club?"

"No," she said, and gestured with her thumb at my father. "I can't leave him."

My father spoke up, and his voice was gentle. "I don't need a babysitter. That's what this amounts to. When Jeff stayed with me tonight, he didn't have to do anything for me—he read and watched television. I don't need someone to be with me." He thought for a minute, then said, "I guess it's so if any-thing happens . . ."

"Right," I said. "But how about if Mom went to the book club in the library, and you came down and sat in the lobby?"

Silence.

I thought about how my father had wanted to go down to dinner, and my mother wouldn't go. "Would you be willing to try breakfast one day a week with Dad?" I asked my mom.

She made some sign of reluctant agreement.

"What about tomorrow?" I said. "Just go one day a week."

"Can't do it tomorrow. Tomorrow the physical therapist comes."

"Mom," I said. "The therapist is coming at ten. Breakfast is from seven to nine. That's just some baloney excuse you're handing me."

She agreed that it was. "But he sleeps in, in the morning!" she said. "I can't get him up!"

"That's not true," he said. "I'm awake in the morning. I lie there because there's noth-ing to get up for."

My mother's mouth was set in a straight

line. I told her, "You know, this is the man who jumped into the ocean to get a letter from you." It's true. During World War II, my father was on the deck of the ship he was stationed to and he opened a letter from my mother, which blew out of his hand. He jumped right into the ocean to retrieve it. When he told me that, I couldn't believe it. "Wasn't that awfully dangerous?" I asked. "Yeah," he said. "I guess I didn't really think about it."

"It seems to me," I told my mother, "that for you to go down to breakfast one day a week with him is not so much of a sacrifice."

At one point in the conversation, my mother said of my father, "Do you think he knows what the doctor said today?"

I looked at my father. "Dad? Did you understand what the doctor said today?"

He turned his blue eyes on me, **What's that?**

"You know when you got tested today?"

"Yeah."

"You . . . you know how you have some memory problems?"

"Right."

"So . . . you took the test, and in some areas you did really well. The numbers, for example, you did better than any of us could have. But in other areas, you seem not to be doing as well. Your memory. But I just want to say that to me, you seem generally better. You're perfectly clear on the phone. Your lungs are better, you were walking really well with the walker. You seem to be in pretty good shape, really."

"I **feel** good," he said, and hope flew around the room and collided with denial.

I took my leave soon afterward, and when I embraced my mother, I said, "I'm sorry I yelled at you."

"It's okay," she said. "I'm getting used to it."

My sister has told her she's wallowing in self-pity. My brother has told her it's selfish of her to expect other people to take her everywhere when she now has other options for transportation. We are all beating the puppy.

The next day, I spoke to my sister, who had taken my mother out shopping. "Did she go down to breakfast with Dad?" I asked. No. She had not.

All these suggestions I make, that others make, too. What do they amount to, anyway? Anne Boleyn, being told she would get to be beheaded by the sword rather than the axe. But life is a minefield at any age. At the VA, I watched a young woman missing a leg try to learn to walk again using the parallel bars, and you could tell it was hard in every way. I saw a young man in a wheelchair yelling out something unintelligible every now and then. He wore a helmet, which I suspected was because he had frequent seizures. Head injury, I thought, another young man who went to war and came home so hurt. He was accompanied by his mother and his wife. His mother was a study in forbearance. His wife was strikingly beautiful, well dressed, her hair up in a complicated arrangement one might see at a prom. Her face was full of sorrow. She pushed her husband in the wheelchair, and then she waited at his side when they stopped. I saw a car pull up for them, and I wondered what they'd do when they got home.

Yes, life is a minefield at any age. Sometimes we feel pretty certain that we know what's coming. But really, we never do. We just walk on. We have to. If we're smart, we count our blessings between the darker surprises. And hope for a fair balance. When I look at my parents' lives, I know they were lucky. And still are.

MAY 1, 2011

At last spring is out in full force. Blossoms abound, nearly painful in their beauty. People are out: joggers, walkers, young mothers pushing baby strollers. I call my mother for an honest discussion, aimed at asking her what she really wants. When I was there, she said in front of my father and me that she accepted the fact that she couldn't go home.

"Well, we should sell the house, then," my father said, and she said, "Not yet." I think her plan is to go back there when her husband dies or is put someplace, and she has talked about him being put someplace where the VA would pay for it, and this enrages my

sister and me. But. We hold only one piece
to a gigantic puzzle.

"You can go back," I told my mother yesterday. "With or without Dad. But you have
to realize that you'll have the same problems
regarding how to take care of yourself there.
Say it's winter, and icy, and you need to take
the trash out to the alley."

"Well, I had begun just leaving the trash
on the porch and Jeff would take it out,"
she said.

My nephew lives a good distance away
from my mother. He helps a great deal, but
he also works at more than one job. Sometimes three.

My mother told me that when she thinks
of home, she remembers it as a serene place.

"It wasn't so serene when you left," I said.
"You were miserable."

What isn't said is that a lot of that misery was from my father losing it. If she were
there alone . . . I don't know, I tell her. She
can decide. If she wants to move back,
she can move back. Right now, we just have
to take this one day at a time.

She mentions that my father won't do

much, not today, not yesterday. His breathing is rapid when he sleeps—does that mean anything? His feet and now his legs are swollen. When I was there, I saw that the nurse had told my mom to switch to frozen vegetables rather than canned, to reduce the sodium in them. "Are you cutting back on his salt?" I ask, and she makes some sort of vague response that means not really. She says it's cold in the apartment, and that she had put a blanket over his feet.

"Is he depressed?" I ask. My sister told me that my mother had told my father he'd been diagnosed with Alzheimer's.

"But why did she tell him?" I asked Vicki.

"She said he asked, but I don't believe her," she said.

Now my mother tells me that my dad saw the book about Alzheimer's that the doctor gave her and asked if he had that. "But I just told him he had memory loss," she says, and I don't believe her either. I think she wants him to know.

I think his lethargy today has to do with him giving up. His depression is fueled by the knowledge that he has Alzheimer's and that things will only get worse.

My mother tells me she's been thinking about the things that my brother and sister and I are telling her. "I made a list of my faults," she said. And I said, "Oh, Mom, we all have so many faults. We're just trying to make our way though this."

She talks again about how she doesn't like it there, how the people are too religious, quoting Bible verses to her all the time. The music they offer is hymns. In retrospect, maybe the other place they looked at would have been better, the one where the bus took them to the casino, the one where they seemed to have more programs, more speakers coming in.

"Maybe we can find the House of Sinners and move you over there," I said, and my mother laughed, and it was so wonderful to hear that.

"Tell me the truth," my mother said. "What did you think of that bingo game we went to?" After my parents moved in, my mother, my sister, and I had gone down for the Saturday night game of bingo, joining the tables full of white-haired people, mostly women, some of whom asked repeatedly, "**What** number did she call?" You got a quarter if you won. Coffee and cookies were served afterward.

"Not my ideal way to spend time," I said. "But it was kind of fun, and it gets you out of the apartment."

I know she thinks the activities at the place are generally infantilizing, and I think she's right. I tell her I'll call the activities director tomorrow to suggest maybe a men's group, and a current events group, something more challenging than what they have in place.

"Well, wait and see what I'm going to do here," my mother says, but I think she knows what she's going to do. She lives with a man who, she told me, is beginning to not recognize people he knows. She revealed that the reason she doesn't want to go to dinner with him is that she's afraid he'll say something to embarrass her.

I said, "But one of the reasons for living there is that you're among your peers. Everybody there has some problem or another. And anyway, I've been with Dad when he's with other people there and he's always just really nice."

But my mother sees my dad as someone who is failing before her eyes. She thinks he might say something inappropriate and his behavior will be associated with her. He cannot tolerate walking far. His memory continues to deteriorate. She said again that she feels as though she is constantly waiting for the other shoe to drop.

"Meaning?" I asked.

"I don't know," she said. But I think she does know. And it will drop soon enough. Yesterday, when we talked frankly about her living without him, I suggested she might miss him more than she knows. They've been married for sixty-eight years.

But what do I know? How do I have the nerve to even open my mouth to say anything about how relationships work when I've always done so poorly in my own? One day I want to slap my mother; the next I want to apologize and apologize and buy her roses and fancy face cream.

"Why do you think that doctor wants to have a family meeting next?" my mother asked.

"Maybe because everything that's happening to you guys is happening to all of us," I said. And she said, "Oh."

Last night, Bill and I went out to dinner to an Indian restaurant, and I kept thinking, **I get to go out to a restaurant for dinner, and it's so** easy. I ordered a Kingfisher beer and took a long swallow and thought about my mother sitting in a chair or maybe at the little desk, making a list of her faults, and I felt suddenly as though my chest had caved in. My eyes filled with tears, and some spilled over. Bill looked questioningly at me and I pointed to my throat. "It's up to here all the time," I said. "My parents. Sometimes it spills over." I laughed, then asked him, "Are there any black stains on my face from my mascara?"

"No," he said. Tenderly.

I wanted to tell him that I needed to go home and have a long cry. Instead I ate more saag paneer, and it was delicious. Later, I learned that Osama bin Laden had been killed, and the first thing that came to me was that I couldn't wait to tell my dad. I imagined him saying, **Who?** not quite remembering who bin Laden was. And if that happened, I was going to tell him who bin Laden was. Patiently. Matter-of-factly. I was going to tell him everything I could, understanding that my own limitations are significant. Breathtaking, really.

Imagine there's a God in heaven. Imagine Him asking everyone who comes, **So. What did you learn in your life?** even as He braces Himself for the answer He knows will come: **Not enough, I guess.**

Out of the blue, or so it seems to my sister and me, my mother decides to meet at the house with a realtor. On a Saturday morning, my sister takes our parents to the meeting, and later she calls me to tell me about it:

When they pull up to the house, they see that the crabapple tree in the backyard is laden with blossoms. The perennials in the garden are coming up. The lawn has been newly mowed; I assume it carries that spiced-green scent. Before my mother even gets out of the car, she says, "I'm coming back." "She **mutters** it," my sister says, "but she mutters loud enough for me to hear."

I imagine my mother feels punched in the stomach, seeing those blossoms on the apple tree, seeing her peonies and lilies rising up in their beds, and her not even there anymore to appreciate them. I imagine it takes more than muscles for her to get out of the car and walk into the house to meet with a realtor who will put a dollar value to something so dear to her. I imagine her swiveling in the seat of the car to better plant her feet on the ground, then using the door handle of the car to hoist herself up and out. I think that as she walks toward the house, her feet might feel numb, and that the air around her might feel insubstantial. I imagine a great confusion in her sympathoadrenal system: she is walking toward something she also wants to run away from.

But my sister tells me that once inside, my mother speaks quite willingly and politely to the realtor, asking the woman—Mary is her name—what she thinks they might get for the house. Mary tells her (gently, I imagine) that the house is dated, but it is a charming house. She thinks they might ask $175–$200,000. And when my sister tells me that, I myself feel punched. It's not enough. I know the realtor knows what she's doing, but it's not enough. I think of a friend of mine who, upon learning that my parents were going to sell, told me, "Don't **you** buy it!" And I thought it was such an odd thing to say, because why would **I** buy it? But my friend knows me better than I know myself, because that is exactly what I thought when I heard the amount. I thought, **Well, hell,** I'll **buy it!** But I can't. I shouldn't. And I won't. Although if I did, I'd rip out the carpet, repaint, fix up the kitchen and the bathroom, take down the PLEASE KNOCK LOUDLY sign on the front door, and voilà.

Vicki tells me that our mother waits upstairs while Mary and my sister go to explore the basement. A little water is down there, leaked in from a window. And I am glad, because it might make my mother think, **Oh, that's right. The maintenance. Do I really want to be responsible for all the maintenance?**

It's hard to think that when my mother was upstairs alone, she didn't walk around, looking in all the empty rooms; and it's hard to think that each room didn't whisper to her. I think it's easier, sometimes, if you can't go back. My mother and I talked recently about how, in some ways, she has too much choice now. If she sells the house, that will be one less thing for her to worry about when she lies in bed at night, awake and fretting, her fingers working as though she is saying the rosary. But if she sells it, it will also be as though she's leaning down and hacking at the roots that have for so long kept her anchored in life as she knows it. And if she doesn't sell the house, she will have to worry about what will become of it, sitting there empty, and how she will continue to afford where she is. And if she moves back into the house, she will not be able to cope, even if my dad does not survive much longer. **You have some choices, and they're all bad! What'll it be?**

Wars come in all shapes and sizes. Battle gear, too. Sometimes it's a khaki uniform and an AK-47. Sometimes it's a cloth coat worn over an aching heart.

When I call my mother later, she tells me about the crabapple tree, about what the realtor said. She doesn't seem to know what to do. She tells me, "Your father is getting worse faster and faster. I wish someone else would spend a month with him. I know you and Vicki don't believe he's as bad as he is."

I want to say, **It's not that. It's just that we don't want you to be cruel to him for something he can't help.** But I know I wouldn't need a month with my dad in the shape he's in to feel like I wanted to pull out my hair. A day or so would probably do it. Maybe a few hours.

I tell her again that I know it's hard. But here we are. "There are no good choices," I tell her. "You just have to kind of pick your poison."

"Well, if something happens to him, or if he goes away," my mother says, "you and your sister have to promise me you won't make me live here."

"You would want to go home?" I ask.

"No, not necessarily."

"A place like the other one we looked at, where the people were a little livelier?"

"Just an apartment, maybe."

"With a mix of people," I say, and she says yes. And I think she's right. I think a mixed-age community is right. As it turns out. While she sits in her "morgue," the lilies at her abandoned house rise up and open to the sun.

It's hard to know how to rescue someone.

It's hard to know how to help them in the way they need to be helped. But I'm learning. We all are.

Meanwhile, my dad's ninetieth birthday is coming up. "Do you want me to order dancing girls?" I ask him.

"Just one will do," he says. "Don't think I could handle two anymore." I feel like we're all of a sudden in an Irish pub pressed up against a mahogany bar, raising a mug to each other. **You still here?** I've asked him, and he has said, **I'm here, I know you, I'm your dad.**

Clink.

MAY 29, 2011

My cousin Patty sends me an email saying
that she has invited my mother and my aunt
Lala to come to Tish's condo to see if they
want any clothes or other things. **They seem
to want to come,** she wrote. And I'm sure
they do. I'm sure, too, that it will be heartbreaking for all three of them.

My first impulse is to say that I'll come,
too. In case my mother needs me. And to bear
witness. I make tentative arrangements to do
that. But after another couple of days go by,
I wonder if it's such a good idea after all. For
one thing, I am suspicious of my writer self,
who surely will exploit this memorial service,
part two. If I go, I won't be able to not write
about it. But there is a difference between

writing about an event to which you are invited and writing about one to which you
invite yourself. My mother going to her late
sister's condo is part of a story I'm trying to
tell. But it belongs to her and not to me. Still,
Lala will have her son to go home to, after
that sad visit. Patty will have her husband.
Who will my mother have? Will my father be
able to help her in the way she needs him to?
Will he be able—that hardest of things—to
leave her alone when she needs to be? When
my parents, my sister, and I all got home
from Tish's funeral, my mother seemed to be
given very little latitude for her grief.

I call my mother to ask if she'd like me to
come. She hesitates, then says, "That would
be too soon." She means I'd be less than a
week away from the day of the family meeting. "I would just come up for the day," I say.
"I'd fly in and out on the same day."

"No," she says. "I'll get through it." And
I don't know if she's objecting to the expense
or if she really doesn't want me to be there.
Maybe she doesn't know that herself.

When I was forty-three, I lost one of my
best friends to breast cancer. One of the
things I remember most is sitting on the little

balcony off her kitchen with her one evening at sunset, looking out over the acres of
land she could see from there, the hills and
the winding roads and the houses nestled
into their lots as though settled on their
mothers' laps. I remember her saying, "I
just want to **be** here." Earlier that day, I'd
sat at the kitchen table and listened while
she spoke to someone on the phone, making her own arrangements for a burial plot.
She told whomever she was speaking to her
name, her address. When she gave her age,
she said, "Well, I'm only forty-four. Which is
really terrible."

Everything was impossible then; every day
brought a new intolerable thing that needed
nonetheless to be tolerated. That phone call
was right after she had told me she would
be going to her parents' house in Arizona to
die, and she told me when I went home that
night to take some things from her place that
she knew I loved: rocks and sea glass she'd
gathered from various beaches, birds' nests,
her cookbook featuring dozens of ways to
prepare chicken breasts. "No," I said. "I'm
not taking anything. Because maybe you'll
get better out there and you'll come back."

We were lying on her bed together, and I was holding on to her and weeping, and she looked around her room and tears came to her eyes. "Yeah," she said. "I don't think I'm coming back, though."

She didn't come back. She died not long after she went to Arizona. Some of her other friends and I were invited to come to her place, to pick up what she had left for us in her codicil. She stipulated that I should have the rocks and the birds' nests because I loved them, and she did, too. Other things were given to me: pottery she'd made, books. I went home with these things and set them around my house just so, and then I sat in a chair in the living room and bawled. Because my having those things meant she really wasn't coming back, and because I had been in her place without her. And every painting on the wall, every lamp and rug and wineglass and perfume bottle, seemed suddenly as though they once had been alive and now were as dead as she was. I had gone to her place that day with a sense of dread, yes, but with an odd kind of excitement, too, feeling somehow that it would be one more chance to visit her. But she wasn't there.

My mother tells me that she's lost some weight and may be able to fit into some of Tish's clothes. "They'll be nice for you to have," I said, wondering if it was true. "As for the knickknacks," my mother says, "there's a little glass coach she had—you know, like a Cinderella coach? I want that. And that's all."

My mother says Patty told her that when she was over at her mom's place, she came across a plastic bag holding something. She looked inside and found the clothes that her mother had worn into the hospital, that place from which she never returned. "She sat right down and cried," my mother said.

"I can imagine," I said. And what I wonder is, would she have wanted anyone with her then? Or, in this age of oversharing, is grief something that we only pretend others can enter into with us? And is that where the consolation is, in the temporary lifting from reality that pretending brings?

JUNE 2, 2011

"He's worse every day," my mother says of my father. Those words seem to be her mantra. But what do they mean, exactly?

"Can you have a conversation with him?" I ask.

My mother thinks about this, then says, "I can have a conversation with him, but then he forgets right away what we talked about."

"Hmm," I say. I'm sitting outside on my back deck on a perfect day: not too hot, not too cold. Next door, a bunch of guys are painting my neighbor's house. I've watched them for days. They are meticulous, thorough, and they seem to enjoy their work. They laugh, call out to one another in Spanish, sing. At lunch, they sit knee to knee on the front porch steps of the house, enjoying the common pleasure of eating with others. These guys are going to paint part of my house that needs repainting, too; we shook on the agreement this morning. There's always something to do when you own a house.

But my parents' house might be sold before it even goes on the market, without our fixing anything. Someone wants to know the instant it becomes available, because her sister, who has two little children just as she does, is moving onto my parents' street, and she would love to live there, too. Chelsea Street. It's a nice name. And it's such a nice idea, the two sisters, the four children, the cycle beginning again.

But.

Something hard-edged rises up in me. "Make sure you ask enough for it," I tell my mother. "You can always come down, but you can't go up."

"Yes," she says. And then, "Well, I guess some decisions are going to have to be made. Maybe when you come."

"Okay," I say.

We talk some more about life there: my dad went to the Wednesday ice-cream social alone, as my mother was tied up with something. When she was out getting her hair done, my dad rode his scooter in the halls. When she asked him how that was, he said, "Boring."

"And you know, he's not supposed to ride that scooter," my mother says. "He's supposed to use the walker."

I want to say, **He's getting out. He's doing something. Who cares if he rides instead of walking? Can't you tell me one good thing about him?**

Instead, "Hmm," I say.

My mother says, "I bring him the crossword puzzle, he won't do it. I bring him tapes and he won't listen to them. He doesn't want to do anything."

"He wanted to go to the dining room for dinner with you," I say. "Have you gone down to dinner with him?"

"I told him I'd go," she says.

"When?" I ask.

"This week," she says. Vaguely.

I think, **When I get up there, I'm taking him out to dinner every night.**

But when my mother says yet again, "I wish someone else could be with him for twenty-four hours and see what this is like," I feel bad for her, too. I feel bad, period.

I hang up from talking to her and sit in my chair, unmoving. Then I ask Bill if he can have breakfast with me at George's Diner. Egg white omelet with spinach and feta, that's what I need. I tell him I'm having a hard time.

"What happened?" he asks.

The little house on the corner of Chelsea and Nebraska. The way that this will all keep on until it comes to a hard finish. The way it's really true that if someone is diagnosed with Alzheimer's they leave long before they leave.

"I . . ." I say. Bill waits. Finally, I say, "It looks like my parents' house is going to be sold. And I'm having a reaction to that that's all out of proportion to . . . I mean, I never even **lived** there."

That's what's in my brain. Those are my words. But as soon as I say them, the veil drops and here comes something else, a memory of me as a little girl, maybe four, asking my dad what his favorite color was. I needed to know. I needed to know **him**, and this would help me. He thought a minute, and

then he said, "I don't know; blue, I guess."
I knew his answer didn't reflect any lack of
willingness or enthusiasm for answering the
question. Rather it revealed something I realized I knew about him instinctively. He loved
all colors. He thought they were all beautiful.
He would pick one, if I asked him to, but
he appreciated them all. He had a slide from
a museum he visited in Holland. It was of a
painting that showed a man's hand holding
a candle in the dark. You could see the red
glow from the blood in the fingers, the black
of the dirt caked into skin folds. The flame
had the deep yellowness of real flame. "**Look**
at that," he said, when he once showed it to
a few people who were gathered in the living room. No one said anything. But I, who
sat in the corner and kept as silent as anyone
else, felt my whole middle self leap up in ac-
knowledgment. It was so close to joy, at first
I thought that was all it was.

JUNE 8, 2011

On the drive to Minnesota for the family meeting, I turn off the radio to listen to the song of the tires on the pavement and let my mind empty into the landscape I'm driving through. Much of that landscape is tedious: freeways and rest stops and billboards and the mud flaps of semis. But there are also gorgeous stretches through Wisconsin: green rolling hills, rock formations so interesting and imposing they could stand in museums. When one makes the necessary pit stops, there is the interesting mix of fellow travelers. You see old people with sunglasses built into visors, teenagers with rainbow-colored hair, babies with Cheerios stuck to their chests, and dogs pulling frantically at their leashes to make pit stops of their own.

I like driving across country alone or, as in this case, in the company of a dog. My four-month-old golden mix, Gabby, is stretched out across the backseat like the Queen of Sheba, and she thinks every idea I have on this trip is fantastic, mostly because the ideas usually involve stopping for food. I like the way time is real time, how you can count down the distance from here to there. And that even though you're not really doing anything, you're doing something.

I'm anxious about this trip, because I fear I'm going to be told my father is worse. I fear he'll be humiliated, confused, saddened. I fear we all will be. I was greatly distracted when I packed this morning, and I'm not sure I brought enough of what I need. But then I tell myself what I always do when I worry about not having what I need when I go on a trip: **Where are you, on the moon? If you need something, you can just buy it there.**

I pull up to my parents' house around seven that night, and my sister arrives almost immediately afterward, to give me the keys to both the house and to my parents' new place. Before she goes home, we get some Chinese take-out at Wong's, and we sit at the booth in the kitchen to eat it. It's so familiar, this booth, this table, this food; there have been so many meals shared here with our parents. Their absence now is like a hulking ghost.

Before I go to bed, I take the dog out. It's such a lovely neighborhood we pass through, full of small, pleasant-looking houses, all of them different from one another. I look into the lit-up windows of the houses I pass, and I see that some of them are still the same as I imagine they were in the thirties, and some have been updated with fine kitchen cabinetry and stone counters, with new windows and doors. Yards and gardens are well tended, seemingly well loved, and are excellent examples of how you can do big things in little spaces. Over and over, I am charmed by what I see people have done, sometimes in spaces not much bigger than a shoe box.

You can walk to the grocery store from this neighborhood, if you're young enough; you can walk to the bookmobile on the days it comes. My mother used to go to the book-mobile every week, and she brought the librarians pecan pralines every Christmas. This served as a bribe, she told me, so that she could move to the top of the list when requesting a popular book.

From this neighborhood, you can walk to the elementary school and the Mexican restaurant and the barber shop and the dollar store and Key's restaurant, where you can get a hot turkey sandwich and a sugar cookie with a diameter roughly equivalent to the planet's. You can walk to Como Park, which has the band shell, where concerts are offered in the summer for free. The park also has the zoo and the kiddie rides and the picnic grounds and the conservatory and the golf course, which is where I now take the dog off the leash and let her run. It's gotten so dark I can hardly pick out Gabby's form as she runs in ever-widening circles, her leash bumping behind her. (This so if I am accused of having my dog off-leash, a ticketable offense, I can say, **Uh-uh, look; she's got it on.**) My white jeans are glowing, as if they're under black light. Gabby is ecstatic with the kind of freedom that is hard to come by in the neighborhood where I live; I imagine she's thinking, **Boy, am I glad we moved** here! Or maybe it's just me, enjoying the fantasy of living here, because that's exactly what I am doing. Also, I'm imagining my parents and how happy they must have felt, moving into a place that offered so much. I'm imagining how when the last box was unpacked, they must have dusted off their hands, thinking that after all those years of traveling around in the military, **there!**—they were finally home, and they would never have to move again.

That night, as I lay in bed, I hear the sounds of the grandfather clock ticking. It can't be; the grandfather clock is in the new place, but I hear it. I stop breathing and I hear it still. And I think, **Fine. A ghost clock. Welcome.** I have always loved the sound of a ticking clock; I love it just as well in phantom form. **Wel-come, wel-come, wel-come.**

"I would like to ask you to do a few things," the occupational therapist—let's call her Janet—says. She's a blond woman with a ponytail, maybe mid-forties, wearing a white coat over her dress, and she has with her another woman, who is a student, there to observe. The student sits in the background and occasionally scribbles furiously away.

Janet shows my father a piece of leather with various kinds of stitching around it: a running stitch, a whipstitch, and a more complicated, overlapping one. "I'll show you a stitch, and then I want you to do it," she says. She does one stitch, and then hands the leather over to my dad. He does a running stitch as well as he can—his compromised

vision is a problem. He's so pleasant and accommodating. "**O**kay," he says; he might
be accepting a mint julep at the Kentucky
Derby. In the way that going out anywhere these days has become an outing—an
occasion—he is in company mode. There is
no apparent embarrassment that a man of
his former might is now reduced to needing
to show someone he can run a large needle
through a large hole. He does not say, **Why
in the world would I ever have to do this?**

No. He could not be more obliging; he
takes the needle, and he does exactly as she
told him. But he skips a hole; then, I think,
another. "Good enough!" Janet says. I look
down, lest my expression give anything away.
He doesn't know he missed holes; he's pleased
that he seems to have done well.

Janet says she won't be giving the test to
dole out pills into a MedMinder; he can't see
well enough to do that. **Or to sew!** I think,
but I recognize my own defensiveness. I'm
the daughter with a virtual slingshot in my
back pocket, looking to deflect from my own
sorrow.

When he first sat down, Janet asked my
dad if he had any hobbies. "Golf," he said.

"But I haven't gotten a chance to go out yet this year." This worried me; my dad hasn't played for years now. He can't see to play. Or walk the required distance.

He said another hobby was that he liked to get out and drive around, but "I'm told I can't do that anymore." He looked over at Janet, and I was wondering if there was faint hope in his heart that she would say, **What? Well, that's not right; of course you can drive around!** Naturally, she didn't say that. She simply smiled and moved on to the skill tests.

Now she brings my father to a wooden wardrobe full of clothes, both men's and women's: a pink fuzzy bathrobe, a tan raincoat, etc. She tells my dad to dress himself as though he were going out on a cold, rainy day. He puts on the raincoat, a hat, and picks out an umbrella from the accessories. Pass.

Next he is asked to "go shopping for a belt." There are rows of belts hung on the wardrobe door, and he is given a wallet with money inside of it. His task is to find a belt that fits and that he can afford, and then pay for it. He looks for the price tag of one belt and reads it with some difficulty: "$9.99," he says. He looks at a few other belts, which are also $9.99. "They're all $9.99," he says, and Janet does not contradict him. He finds one that fits, then goes to the wallet to pay for it. Not enough money is in the wallet; he'll have to go back to shopping. At first, he is a bit confused: Aren't all the belts $9.99? But Janet guides him into looking further, and he discovers a cheaper belt, which he then pays for. Good enough. Janet takes the money back and my dad says, "Oh, I don't get to keep it?"

"Everybody tries to pull that on me," Janet says, laughing, and I'm relieved she recognized that he was joking.

My father is now asked to choose things from a box of disparate items in order to wash his hands. He picks up the soap but is at a loss as to how he is meant to **really** wash his hands; he hasn't noticed that there's a sink across the room. He is directed to it and he washes his hands thoroughly, then dries them well.

He is brought to a kitchen-like area of the room and asked to toast a piece of bread, butter it, and put jam on it. "No plug," my dad says, and Janet, pleased, says, "Right!"

and carries the toaster to another part of the room, where my dad plugs it in. He puts the bread in the toaster, and when it pops up, it's not brown. He puts it in again, and the same thing happens. He looks over at Janet, play-exasperated, and she says, "Okay, well, let's finish up." He puts the toast in for a third time, and this time it pops up brown. And then he butters it, puts the jam on. **A+,** I think, but this will turn out to be not so. She will take points off for him trying to brown the toast again instead of buttering it, even though I try to politely argue that what he did was completely logical, that it is what I would have done, too. I say, "You know, I think if you had said, **It's okay that it's not brown, just go ahead and finish preparing the toast**, he would have gone to the butter right away." She stares coolly at me and says, "These are standardized questions." **Then standardize your toaster so that it** toasts, I want to say, but don't.

My dad takes a map test, which requires him to find his way around the corridors outside the room; this he does very well. Then he and the therapist sit down to calculate his average. Janet tells him he got four out of five on this test, three out of five on that, and so on. Then she grabs her calculator to figure out his average, but before she finishes entering the first number, my father says, "Four point six," and he's exactly right. Janet looks over at him. "You're good at this," she says. My sister and I look at each other triumphantly.

In the family meeting with the doctor, my brother, back home in Hawaii, is on the speakerphone as we all discuss what's next. One of the things that comes up is that a social worker will be calling my mother to try to help get my dad into an adult daycare program at the VA twice a week. "I'll have to think about that," my father says. "Transportation is a problem."

"They'll come and get you," Janet says.

"We'll see," my dad says, and now it's my mother and I who exchange glances, worried ones. My dad has got to do this, to give my mother some relief. She is so frazzled and worn out, she has no patience left. I'm not sure anyone would. Still, my sister and I gossip about her, the way she scowls when he kisses her good morning. "Would it kill her to go down to dinner with him?" we ask each other. "He took care of **her** for so **long**!" But it's like that old argument about how your parents took care of you when you were a baby; now it's your turn. It's not the same. Baby butts are **cute.**

When it's my mother's turn to speak, she complains that she gives my father cross-word puzzles to do, Sudoku puzzles to do, but he won't do them. "He can't!" Janet says, in a way that sounds more than just a little peeved. She says, "It's frustrating to try to do something you used to be able to do and just can't do anymore!"

My mother looks down at her hands.

I inspect my own.

My brother is saying nothing, and when the doctor asks him if he has anything to add, he says, "Hi, Dad," and in those two words it's like he's come into the room, taken my father away from the table, looked into his eyes, and said, "Whew! They're raking you over the coals a little bit, aren't they?" My brother talks about how maybe what my dad needs is a nice motorcycle ride with him. We all smile, and I think it's a pretty safe bet to think that we're all wishing it could be so. But those days are over, and we need to deal with the situation at hand. Not long ago, I am embarrassed to admit, I told my mother, "Each stage of life comes with its own challenges." As if she doesn't know that. It was uncommon courtesy and grace that kept her from shaking her head and walking away from me.

When it's my turn, I say that it would be helpful if my father would stop following my mother around. She goes to do the laundry and here he comes down the hall, looking for her. She visits the woman next door, same thing. She goes to the lobby to fetch the mail and stops briefly to talk to someone in the hall, and he's ready to put out an APB.

I called my mother once and she moved into the bathroom to talk. We were discussing something we didn't want my dad to hear: whether or not we should say the words **Alzheimer's disease** to him again, whether that might help him to understand some things that were happening, or if it would only make him feel worse. But, "I have to go," my mother said suddenly. "He's standing right outside the door."

"She just needs a little break now and

then," I say. "If my dad could just give her ten, twenty minutes."

Janet looks at me. "He **can't.**"

All of a sudden, I get it. His not doing puzzles is not lack of will but lack of ability. This man who uncomplainingly stayed home by himself while his wife went on vacations with her sisters, or spent whole days out shopping with them, now can't go any length of time without wondering where she is, worrying about whether or not she's all right. Time is not the same reliable index it was before; it's now loose and vaguely incomprehensible. Either my mother is there or she is not. When she's not, he doesn't know how long it's been since he's seen her.

Well, I'm an Army brat, used to constant change and upheaval. When I'm with him, I'll move again, this time into the land of Time As He Knows It. When I'm with him and my mother is gone and he asks repeatedly, "Where's your mother?" I'll tell him. And each time, I'll try to act as if he's asking me for the first time. I'll tell him where she is, how long she's been gone, and when she might be expected to return. I'm not only an Army brat, I'm a mother. I know some ways of soothing. I know that no matter what the problem or fear, it helps to say in some way or another, **Everything will be all right**.

I don't want to think about this, but I can't help it: when my first golden, Toby, was very sick—was dying— he needed to go out. He bounded down the back stairs, not understanding the extent of his weakness. When he came back in, he couldn't make it to the spot in the living room where he liked to sleep. He collapsed in the kitchen, in front of the refrigerator. And I lay on the floor beside him, saying, "You need to stay here, pal? Okay, we'll stay here together." We lay there for some time, and the thing I remember most is that it wasn't so bad. It was just different. The main thing was, he was still alive, and we were together. Also, it was convenient, lying there, in case either of us wanted something from the fridge. Toby was particularly fond of cheese.

❖

That evening, I want to take my parents out to dinner, and I ask them to tell me someplace they'd like to go. "Well, we like Little Venice," my mother says. "But that's really far away."

"No problem, we'll go there," I tell her. I'm thinking, **You want to go to San Francisco for dinner? Listen, I've got some time on my hands, and it belongs to you.**

Easy to make such grandiose gestures in thought. And anyway, the time it takes to drive to Little Venice? About eight minutes. It's good food. The atmosphere is homey; we might be in someone's kitchen. A member of the family who owns the place comes over to our table to see what we thought of the food. "It's really **good**," I say. "Well, of course it is," she says. She points to my mother's half-empty (huge) platter. "Box?" she asks.

After dinner, we drop by the house so that I can pick up my dog; I left her there while we had dinner. I'm a little afraid to bring my parents in, afraid it will make them sad, but they want to come in with me. I can't tell from their behavior if being there bothers them or not. But later, after I've brought them back to the apartment, I ask my mother if, when she saw the house, she still wanted to go back. "In the worst way," she says, and I can think of absolutely nothing to say in return.

Before I leave their apartment to go back to the house for sleep, my mother asks me to look through a box of Aunt Tish's clothes that she salvaged, to see if there's anything I want. I find some casual tops, and a soft gray jacket that feels like being embraced. That's the thing I put on right away, and I keep on for nearly all the rest of my stay there.

⚙

On Friday I awaken to a gray, rainy morning. I start some coffee and sit in the booth, waiting for it to finish. I look around the kitchen at all the choices my mother made when she redecorated. She got a number of new outlets, so she didn't have to move things to plug them in anymore. She refused a dishwasher, opting for more cupboard space, and got a number of pull-out shelves and clever storage spaces. She eliminated the wallpaper and selected a crème-café-colored paint. She got a double sink, a nice faucet, a remodeled booth. "Your mother is spending your inheritance!"

my father complained, but I said, "Spend it! Spend it **all**. Why don't you take a cruise?"

They didn't take a cruise. My mother got the kitchen she wanted, and now she has left it behind.

When the coffee is done, I pour a cup, and then sit at the table, crying. I am suddenly overwhelmed with remorse about this house going on the market, about it being lived in by strangers. I remember my father carving the Thanksgiving turkey and the Easter ham on the pull-out cutting board, newspaper spread out below him to catch the juices and the occasional pieces of meat that fell, much to the delight of whatever dog was there— and there was almost always a dog there, if not one that belonged to my parents, then one that belonged to my sister or me.

I remember bringing my now thirty-six-year-old daughter over here a couple of times a week, when I lived in Minneapolis and worked the evening shift as a nurse. My mother would keep two-year-old Julie until my husband could pick her up. I've seen every season in this house, year after year: the apple tree bare, then budding, then flowering, then greening, then dropping its leaves to begin the cycle all over again. Though I never really lived here, this house has been the single most constant place in my life. My parents lived here for four and a half decades; I've come back to it again and again for the same length of time.

I look out into the yard, which, absent its container garden, fountain, birdbath, grill, and patio furniture, seems so much smaller. It's hard to think that so many of us once fit out there when we had outdoor family gatherings.

I think of how I brought certain men to this house, including my college boyfriend, Joel, whom my mother adored, not least because he looked like a young Gregory Peck. I brought Joel along when I came to tell my parents that I was going to drop out of college. They were surprised, angry, disappointed, and I stood in this very kitchen weeping on Joel's chest, saying, "See? I told you they wouldn't understand!" I was the only one in the family to go to college; when I dropped out, I took a lot away from my parents. College wasn't the place for me; I wanted the world to be my classroom, but they didn't understand how I could squander what they saw as such an opportunity.

I also brought my boyfriend John here. He was the keyboard player in the band I was in; we moved out to California together, driving a taxi-yellow van that had owosso TYPEWRITER COMPANY stenciled on the side. Before we left, we came over to say goodbye to my parents. My mother was furious that I was moving to California, and would not come out to say goodbye or anything else to me. My dad did, though. He hugged me and said goodbye, and he told John that if anything happened to me, he would come looking for him with a gun. John said, "Yes, sir." When we drove away, my father stood with his arms resting along the top of the fence, watching us go. Over the years, he always watched me leave that way, standing at the fence, his arms crossed over the top rail. When it became hard for him to see, he still watched. When it became hard for him to walk, he accompanied me as far as the back door, then, from the window, watched me go.

I push back the rush of memories and think instead about where we all are now. I think maybe Mom could start a newspaper at the new place. Maybe Dad could join the men's discussion group. Maybe there is a way to enrich their lives and fill in the gap that leaving this house has made.

Early that afternoon, Lois, an old friend who lives in Minneapolis, comes over. She was my roommate in 1967–68, when we were going to the University of Minnesota, and we had a studio apartment (rent: $65 a month, split) where the bathroom was shared with four boys who lived in the apartment next to us. What a time that was! Many mornings, I made breakfast for all of us before we headed out for class, feeling like a real mother hen. The boys and Lois and I had a shaving cream fight that was nothing short of magnificent, running back and forth between apartments. They banged on their walls when they'd had enough of Lois and me playing our guitars and harmonizing; we banged on the bathroom door to get them out when we needed in. And we stuffed toilet paper into the keyhole of the bathroom door so they couldn't spy on us when we were in there.

But Lois comes over, and we take Gabby for a two-hour walk. It's longer than we anticipated, mostly because we get a little lost.

But it's fortuitous; we get to have a good long talk about aging and the problems it brings. Then we talk about how Lois is planning to leave her Minneapolis home to live with her daughter and family in Denver.

"But you love Minneapolis!" I say.

She nods. "Yes. I do."

"Are you **sure** you want to live with your daughter?" I ask, and she looks wearily over at me. "Oh, I don't know what I want," she says. "But I can't afford the house anymore."

We have spent a long time talking about problems with our parents: the financial drain, the emotional drain, the time drain. But here come the issues of aging that **we** will face, nipping at our heels. And our kids won't be able to help us the way we are helping our parents; the economy won't allow it. We find ourselves in the same position as so many others, helping both our parents and our children. Right now, I feel that it's an honor, truly; I'm happy to do it. I feel lucky I **can** do it. But I can see that a time may come when I deeply resent it, when my fears about how I will care for myself will have me closing my wallet against helping anyone else. We spend a fair amount of time talking about the Black

Pill. We realize we each know what to do, if it comes to that.

And then we can't bear it anymore, and we turn our attention to the blue herons who stand regally on one leg, the egrets dunking their heads to go fishing, the spring flowers struggling against the rain to make their presence known, the Baltimore oriole calling out from his post high up in the branches. We admire the placid water of the lake, the dip of the willow tree's leaves into it, the blue-green coves created by hanging boughs. We smile at the Canada geese goslings who have grown past puffball stage and into an endearing gawkiness. We take what we can from nature, which never ages, but rather offers constant beauty and solace to those who will take the time to see it. I remember this about Lois and me: that we both always found what we needed in nature. And we shared other things, too. We fell asleep to music every night: Lou Rawls. Odetta. Buffy Sainte-Marie. Lois once broke up with a boyfriend just because I had broken up with mine and she figured I could use the company. Late one winter night we went out with our coats over our pajamas in order to give our Christmas tree a late-night Viking funeral: we set it on fire, ornaments and all, and dumped it off a railroad bridge into the Mississippi River. Then we probably went home and had some scotch, and I probably put Coke in mine.

When we get back to my parents' house and part ways, we laugh, embracing (what can you do?), and wish each other luck.

I leave the worn-out dog in the house and go over to get my parents. I take them to Best Buy, where I'm going to get my mother a freezer. It's meant to appease my mother's desire for more storage for food, thereby making the place she's living in now more appealing to her. But my father doesn't understand why we're getting a freezer. "Why do we need it?" he asks, and my mother tells him that the frozen pizzas she likes to buy won't fit into the little freezer on top of the fridge, and she wants to be able to stock up on things that come on sale. My father shakes his head, clearly disgusted at what he sees as unnecessary expense. "We have two of **every**thing," he says. And my mother finally gives up. With tears in her eyes, she tells him, "Oh, never mind, then." And to me, "I knew he'd do this."

"No," I say. "We're getting you your freezer." I speak to my dad firmly, telling him that this is something we have all discussed, though the truth is that mostly my sister and mother and I have discussed it. I call over a salesperson; I make arrangements on the phone with my sister's husband to bring the freezer to my parents' apartment in his truck. When we are waiting for the paper-work to be complete, my dad gets restless. I leave my mother in the waiting area, and take my dad for spin—he's in one of the store's wheelchairs. I show him the 3D televisions. "Doesn't it look like things are coming right at you, like you can just reach out and touch them?"

"Yeah, it does," he says, but he wearies of what is essentially just another gimmick, and we wander down this aisle and that. Fi-nally, we are ready to go, and we ride home in silence.

That evening, my parents and I are meant to have dinner with another couple, Russell and Dee Fate, who just moved from Chicago to the residence where my parents are now. I met Russell yesterday out in the hall—it seems you are always meeting people out in the hall at that place. A resolutely cheerful man who used to be a pastor, he was ambling along, hunched over his walker. He told me they'd had to leave their house in Iowa and a lot of friends behind, but . . . the children were here. Ah, I said. Yes. A whole story in those four words, a story I was beginning to know very well.

At one point, I asked Russell something, and he fumbled with the answer; it was a memory issue of some kind. "It is . . . it is, uh . . ." he said. And then, most affectingly, he looked right at me and said, "I want to be honest about this." He was referring, I think, to the difficulties he was having mentally. And physically, I suppose. Without talking about it directly, I gathered that what Russell and his wife had decided to do was to openly admit to their inabilities and face whatever lay ahead with as much love and optimism as possible, waiting for gifts of grace. (I saw him days later out in the hall wearing rainbow-colored suspenders, and when I complimented him on them, he said, "Yes, they make me feel good.")

On the day we met, I told Russell my parents were new, too, and maybe he and his wife and my parents and I could all have dinner together the next night in the dining room. "Oh," he said, "that's a wonderful idea!" and a particular light shone in his eye. I got his phone number, called later to confirm with his wife ("Well, what a wonderful idea!" said she), and then I taped their phone number to my parents' refrigerator. **Here you go: friends! See??**

Just before it's time to go downstairs to meet Russell and Dee in the lobby, my dad comes into the kitchen wearing a nice shirt and pants and his fancy cuff links, comb marks in his damp hair. "You changed clothes!" my mother says, and he says, "Yeah, I did."

"Well, I didn't," she says, and he says she doesn't have to; **he** just wanted to. He puts his hand up to his face and says, "Oh. I forgot to shave."

"You don't have to shave," my mother says, but my father says yes he does, and he disappears into the back to go into his bathroom. My mother seems annoyed that he's taking such pains, but I'm thrilled. I hear the buzz of his razor and it's a happy sound to me. Hopeful.

We get to the lobby at the agreed-upon time, and there's no sign of Russ and Dee. We wait a little longer—five minutes, ten—and finally I go and knock at their door. I'm greeted with great pleasure by Russell, who, when I remind him about our dinner plans, says, "Oh! We forgot!" He calls out to his wife that I am there. She comes to the door, a gentle-looking woman, tall and thin with soft blond hair. "I'm afraid we forgot," she says, smiling but shame-faced. "I'm so sorry."

"No problem," I say. "But would you like to come now?"

"Oh, sure, of course!" she says. "Wonderful!"

We are seated together at a large round table, and soon my father is engaged in conversation with Russ, and my mother with his wife. Russ asks my father what he finds to do around there, and my father says, "Not much. Mostly sit on my butt!" But he laughs saying it, and Russ laughs with him. My mother asks Dee if she likes baseball (my mother is a rabid Twins fan), and Dee says no, she's more for tennis. I sit still as a stone, afraid to say or do anything that might interfere with this fragile beginning.

Finally, I come up with some excuse, leave the table, and go up to my parents' apartment. About twenty minutes later, they come back. My mother's spirits seem improved, and my father says, "Well! That was a nice evening."

On Saturday morning, I call my mother from the grocery store. I tell her I'll make dinner for us tonight: lemon-garlic chicken, mashed potatoes, green beans, spinach-strawberry salad, an apple pie. "Oh," she says, sounding pleased. In addition to groceries, I buy her a five-dollar betting card. Deluxe.

When I get to the apartment, I see that my mother's in a bad mood. The toilet backed up last night, and she cleaned the mess with a mop, then with towels, which she had to wring out and carry down to the laundry room.

"What made it back up, I wonder?" I say, and my mother answers in the tired and aggrieved voice I am beginning to get used to. "Oh, Lucille [her neighbor] says it happens all the time."

"But this is the first time for you," I say, and she reluctantly agrees.

"And there is a handyman here who can fix it," I say.

"On **Mon**day," she says.

"On Monday, yes," I say, and do not add, "At least now you have two bathrooms."

My sister and I are going to take my father out to lunch and to get him some new pants, which he says he doesn't need, but he does—his old ones are hanging off him. We schedule the day as we would a toddler's: first, we'll find a restaurant close to the store where we're going and feed him, so he'll have enough stamina to try on clothes. Vicki picked a small men's store where there would be a big selection and where someone would actually wait on you.

When we get to the mall, I ask my dad, "Would you like to go to a soup-and-sandwich place for lunch?"

"What's your mother going to eat?" is his response.

My sister and I look at each other. "Mom

has a sandwich all made," I tell him. "She'll eat that. She's all set."

"Okay," he says, and it is in that gentle and accommodating tone that I am getting used to. He used to be the yeller and my mom the soft-spoken one. Now she's the yeller, though her yelling is quiet, which is worse.

We eat lunch on the patio of the sandwich place, and my sister feeds the birds crumbs from her sandwich, and my dad does, too. Put any animal in front of my dad or my sister or me and we will cotton to it.

After lunch, we head to the men's store, and my father is put into a dressing room. It's arduous for him, pulling off trousers and pulling them on, but finally he is given something that fits well, and we buy him the same kind of pants in two different colors. I point to a shirt that I think would look nice on him, but my sister shakes her head—he'll just refuse, and anyway, he's good on shirts. However. He likes the shirt I found, too. We walk out of the store with two pairs of pants and two shirts, one a kind of floral Hawaiian one that's just for fun and that I tell my dad he'll look swell in when he's sitting out in the gazebo.

"Okay," he says.

We've tried to stay gone for as long as we can so as to give my mom a break, but we've reached our limit; our dad is visibly tired.

When we get back to the apartment, my mother is sitting on the sofa, sleeping. She awakens when we're right behind her. My dad sits close beside her; he missed her.

"Anything happen when I was gone?" he asks.

My mother snorts. "Yeah. **Right**."

My sister and I look at each other. My dad says nothing more.

The plan now is for my sister to take my mother to the grocery store. One of the reasons we picked this residence is that there are free buses that go to two grocery stores and to Target, which also has groceries. But my mother wants to go to her old grocery store, so my sister takes her there. Every Saturday, after having worked at her full-time job that more often than not requires overtime, my sister takes my parents to see my father's brother in the nursing home, and then she takes my mother to get groceries. Every Saturday. (Last time she took my mother to the store, my dad came along because he can no longer be left alone. While my mother lingered—and lingered—over the dairy department, my father asked my sister, "What is she **do**ing?" And my sister said, "Just leave her alone, Dad, she likes to take her time.")

We have a nice dinner that night, and my father is very complimentary, inviting me to move in with them and sleep on his sofa and be his personal chef. He has agreed to play bingo with me that evening, and so right after dinner we head downstairs, he and I, and my sister stays with my mother to help her clean up.

We arrive late to bingo; they've begun playing already, but we are given cards and chips by a very kind person who welcomes us there, late or not. Soon we are playing opposite two ladies who seem not all that friendly; they don't say much and their expressions are dour. There are different varieties of games that are played here: four corners, coverall, the letter **T**. The formation for whatever they're playing is put up on a sample card off to the side of the room. My dad can't see that far; indeed, he has trouble seeing the large numbers on the bingo card before him, so I make up a sample card to put right next to him. "See this?" I tell him quietly. "This time, we're making the letter **T**."

He keeps playing regular bingo, though, and I don't want to keep correcting him. But then he shouts out excitedly, "Bingo!" when he has made a straight line across. Kay, who's calling the numbers, asks him to repeat, to confirm the win. "It's . . . We had a false alarm," I tell her. My father looks at me, confused. "They're making the letter **T**," I tell him again.

"Oh," he says, and he is visibly embarrassed. But at that moment I feel the whole room warm in sympathy. The women we sit across from gentle their expressions and talk about how it's hard, sometimes, to keep up with what's happening, hard to see the chips, the numbers. And my dad stays and tries again. Later, he wins for real. Twenty-five cents feels like a million dollars.

My sister and I have agreed to help my father fill out the forms for a living will, and that's the last thing on the list for today. After my dad and I return from bingo, we get started. My mother won't help him do it because she doesn't agree with his choices. "I had one he filled out that said what I think it should," she told my sister, and Vicki said, "This isn't about you. It's about what he wants now."

My father, my sister, and I sit at the dining room table to fill out the forms. Every time my dad answers affirmatively to wanting measures to be taken, my mother mutters angrily. One question begins, "If you are incapacitated mentally with Alzheimer's disease or some other . . ." Here my mother mutters, "Like you are **now**?"

She is in the kitchen, puttering around, when she makes this remark and I glare at her back. "**Excuse** me?" I say.

She says nothing.

"Mom. Did you have something you wanted to say?" I ask.

Nothing.

At one point, my father is meant to list the people who should be charged with the decision about whether to pull the plug. He has decided that if there's any hope for improvement, he wants to be kept alive, unless it makes for financial hardships. My mother, on the other hand, wants no measures taken at all for any reason. When I was trying to explain to my dad what this question meant,

I said, "For this question, what you need to decide is how much you want done to keep you alive and under what circumstances. Basically, if Mom gets a hangnail, she wants us to kill her. But how about you?" (Three of us smiled at a not-very-good joke.)

Earlier, when I thought of filling out these forms, I imagined—hoped for—a kind of flavored-coffee commercial scenario: my sister and I helping my dad with tenderness and humor as sun streamed through a window, as bluebirds sang outside. Difficult questions, perhaps, but good ones. Necessary ones. And, in my imagination, when we completed the forms we would be both relieved and bound a little closer in love. I had no idea the questions would often be so utterly confusing, or that my mother would be fuming in the background, as though in our helping her husband, as she'd asked us to do, we were conspiring against her. It reminded me of a friend who told me about her mother and sister, who live together and like different movies (no surprise there). When the daughter recently put on a movie she'd rented that the mother didn't like, the mother told my friend, "It was just a slap in the face!"

Now, after being asked if it's okay if his three kids make the decision to pull the plug—and by the way, we must all be in agreement with one another—my father looks at us in confusion, then turns in his chair, seeking out his wife. "Shouldn't your mother be involved in this decision?"

"I won't," my mother says, at the same time that I say, "She doesn't feel she can, Dad, because her beliefs about this situation are so different from yours. So Jeff, Vicki, and I will be the three, okay?"

"Okay," he says.

I'm going home the next day. Before my sister and I leave my parents' apartment that night, I ask my mother if she will honor my father's request to go downstairs to dinner. "Just one night a week," I say. "Can you do that, just one night a week?'

"We'll see," she says.

"And he would like to go down to breakfast, too," I say. "How about breakfast one day a week. It's free!"

"You have to sign up for the Sunday brunch, and it's too late to do that now," she says.

"How about Monday?" I say.

"The nurse comes Monday."

"Tuesday?" I say.

She stands there. She has no excuse to offer, but she won't say yes.

My sister leaps out of her chair. "Jesus Christ!" she says, and leaves the apartment.

When I am on my way out a few minutes later, my mother says, "I suppose Vic's mad at me."

"Well, it's frustrating, Mom," I say. "It doesn't seem like so much to ask, that you would go downstairs for breakfast one time a week."

And now my mother explodes. "You people just **leave me alone**!" she says, through clenched teeth. "I'll send you a check for the freezer, and you just **leave me alone.**"

"Okay," I say lightly, and hug my father goodbye.

After I close the door, I stand listening, and I hear my father say, "You want me to leave you alone?"

"Not you," my mother says. "**Those** two! 'You do this, you do that!' I'm going to send her a check for the goddamn freezer, and I want them to leave me **alone**!"

I walk quickly down the hall. I'm glad

I'm going home tomorrow. I think about my friend Marianne, who is dealing with problems all the time with her mother, who is suffering from dementia. Last time I spoke to Marianne, she said, "Every day it's like Anything Can Happen Day on **The Mickey Mouse Club**."

I find my sister in the hall and we talk about how my mother has said she won't weigh in on my father's care if he can't make decisions for himself; we talk about how mean she is to him, how we are sick of her chronic bad moods and spitefulness, her muttering and unwillingness to just **try**, her ingratitude for all that is done for her. "If she sends you a check, cash it," my sister says.

"I can't do that," I say.

"Well, keep it, at least," Vicki says. "Let her think you cashed it."

"Okay," I say, but I think we both know it's highly unlikely any such check will appear.

I'll be back on Friday for my father's ninetieth birthday. My uncle Frank recently said he wished he could go back to the old neighborhood, to see the house where he and my dad were born. We decided that on my dad's birthday, we'd take them both there;

the house is still standing. We asked my dad and he said yes, he'd like to do that. My sister says she'll find a handicap van so that he can roll right in. Frank's son wants to come, and will follow in his car. My mother is not coming. That way she can have some time alone. **You're welcome.**

"How you parents?" Mary, the woman who cleans my house once a week, asks. Mary and I talk about almost everything: Men. Children. Our waistlines. Politics. Recipes. Once when she came, I had a shower cap on my head, some egg-and-honey mixture on my hair. "My hair is getting so thin!" I said, and she said, "Me, too!" and pulled strands of hair out from the sides of her head. "My hair used to be so thick!" I said, and she said, "Me, too!"

"Egg yolks are supposed to help," I told her. "Yes," she said, "my friend put." "Coconut milk is supposed to help, too," I said. "Oh, yes?" she asked. I nodded solemnly and then I said, "I don't **really** know.

I just read it in a magazine. Basically, we're just getting old. **I** am, anyway." "Me, too," she said, and sighed. "We need to get rid of all our mirrors," I said, and she laughed and I did, too, and though I guess it's impossible, I do think it's an excellent idea. Imagine how freeing that would be, and how much fun to see everyone walking around with poppy seeds stuck between their teeth. What a great equalizer that would be.

But today, when Mary asks, "How you parents?" I tell her the truth.

She nods, then says, "In Poland, we say old people like trees. Not like to move." She looks down at her feet, as if there are roots there.

"I know," I say. "But they had to."

"Yes," she says. And then we both get to work.

Later in the day, I call my mother and she tells me she wrote down "what you people think of me. Maybe someday I'll show it to you." I would like to see it, but I don't know how to say those words to her. What I would mean is, **I would appreciate your telling me the truth.** What she would hear, I fear, would be something else.

She tells me she tried to call the Alzheimer's Association and my father "had a fit." I can't quite understand what he had a fit about, but she says he had a fit. So I say I'll call.

For relief later that day, I take a walk with Gabby through my neighborhood, relieved that it's my neighborhood, far away from the places I've been. I see a little girl walking along with a dollar bill folded over in her hand. A woman licking an ice-cream cone. A guy making a scalloped edge for the garden. Two teenage girls on a bike, one on the seat, the other pedaling. I try to sneak Gabby into the library and the security guard stops me. He points to her. "Is that a . . ."

"Service dog?" I say.

"Yeah."

"Sort of."

"She can't come in," he says.

"I'm afraid to leave her outside. She's just a puppy."

The guard is unmoved.

"All I have to do is pick up a book I reserved," I say. "I'll be so quick."

"All right, but **just this once**," the guy says. He's in a wheelchair, and has some kind of disability, maybe cerebral palsy. I like taking orders from him. It's nice to see that someone who might under other circumstances be helpless can now be in a position of authority.

The next day, I call my mother and she says she tried to take my dad to breakfast but he refused. When he heard that "this hotel" did not serve bacon and eggs, and that he would have to wait in line for breakfast rather than be served, he didn't want to go.

"Okay, well, at least you tried," I say.

The truth is, I'm suspicious about how she tried. I imagine her standing over him, saying, **It's much earlier than you usually get up, but if you want breakfast you'll have to get ready right now. We'll have to go down and stand in line forever for that god-awful oatmeal. No doubt all the rolls will be gone, so don't count on having them. And you know, that's all they have, is rolls and oatmeal. And weak coffee.**

"At least you tried," I say again.

It's my father's ninetieth birthday. I'm driving up to Minnesota again, and this time Bill is coming with me. There's a dinner tonight at a restaurant my parents like, and Vicki and her husband, Derk, will be joining us. We arrive at my parents' apartment just before it's time to go to the restaurant.

My mother comes out of her bathroom and points to her fancy black flowered blouse, saying, "Tish is joining us for dinner."

"Good," I say. And then, "You look nice!"

My father is dressed up, too, and seems genuinely excited about going out. For one moment, it's like opening a door to a better time: my parents dressed up, going out for the evening. Period.

The restaurant seats us at a square table where it will be nearly impossible for my father to hear. I think about asking for a round table, where he seems to do better, but then I see that he is settling right in; he's used to this. He won't be able to hear? So what? He is out to dinner with his family, seated next to his wife, who is wearing a pretty blouse and dangly black-and-gold earrings and is in possession of the same dimples that practically killed him dead when he first met her. He has his light-up magnifying tool to peruse the menu. He is wearing a suit and he walked in the restaurant by himself and will walk out of the restaurant by himself. He will go home after dinner and sleep in his own bed. His cup runneth over.

When the waitress appears, my father looks up at her and, really rather expansively, I think, says "I'll have an old-fashioned."

In keeping with the theme, I order a Bacardi cocktail. When it comes, I taste it, and it's awful. But what care I? I'm out to dinner with my family. I can read the menu. I can drive home. I'll have someone to talk to before I fall asleep. My cup runneth over, too.

Goodness and mercy may not follow me all the days of my life, but it is here now.

Someone once told me she thought of life as being stuck inside an airless little cabin, constantly near asphyxiation. But every now and then a rush of fresh air came under the door and kept her alive. And I told her it seemed clear to me that everyone's job was to get on the floor and lie right by that crack.

On Saturday morning, I stand in the kitchen with my mother, talking about Vicki, Bill, and me taking my father and his brother to their birthplace. I confirm that she does not want to come, so that she will get time alone. But when I say, "Okay, then, you're not invited," as a kind of joke, it comes out unnecessarily cruel.

We meet a handicap van at the nursing home, and Frank is wheeled into it, in high spirits. He's offering us his wide smile, and despite his missing teeth, it's a beautiful smile, a light-up-the-room kind.

And then we're off, taking the scenic route

through the park. We've had to hire a driver for the van, and he's a cheerful and accommodating man. He is also, as we will come to see, a man who notices things, who pays attention. He chats with my sister, who's riding in the seat beside him. I'm sitting in the back with my father and my uncle. They stare out the window, and I wonder how much they're able to see, or if there isn't some pleasure just sitting in a moving vehicle, going past things, even if what they see is only blurs of color and texture. Their silence, their stillness, seems to indicate so.

When we get to the old neighborhood, my dad starts naming all the people who used to live on this block: he remembers the name of virtually every family on both sides of the street. There used to be barns in some backyards, he tells us. His father, a teamster, kept horses in the backyard; chickens, too. There is a FOR SALE sign on the house, a lockbox on the door, and Vicki and I decide to call the realtor to see if there's any way we can get in. Vicki will explain it's my dad's ninetieth, that this is the house he and his brother were born in; maybe she'll let us in. The realtor tells us she has no time to meet us, but she gives us the code to the lockbox—the house is empty; I suppose she figures there will be minimum risk. Also, she has a heart.

After some arduous manipulation that finally requires lifting Frank's wheelchair—with him in it—into the house, there the brothers are, in the little kitchen of the house where they were born, my father ninety years ago, my uncle over ninety-five. My father says, "Bill [the oldest brother, long deceased] used to make us dance with the broom in this kitchen. You know, to clean it up." He wanders into another room off the kitchen and stands there. "Bedroom," he says, and I can only imagine the memories that must be washing over him: he and his brothers and sister as children, both of his parents alive.

He walks over to stand at the top of the stairs that lead down to the basement. "I fell down these steps once," he says, peering down as if expecting to see the ghost of his boy self lying there, more chagrined than injured. I move beside him and put one hand on his arm. I say, "Yeah, well, don't be falling down them again." He smiles and moves away, wanders in and out of the rooms a few times over. The house has been done over and it's quite nice now. The kitchen and bathroom have been tastefully modernized; there's a charming pantry that probably was there when my father lived there, freshly painted in a soft white. The wood floors are exposed and polished, the lighting fixtures are well chosen. There is a cozy Pottery Barn feeling to the place.

"It hasn't really changed much," my father says. "No," Frank says. My sister and I look at each other and smile.

Our next stop is White Castle, per Frank's request. We seat the brothers at a table and go up to the counter to order. When I turn around, I see that my father's hand is on his brother's back. I ask someone to take a picture: to capture the view from behind of those two old men, but by the time a camera is produced, my father has taken his hand away. Still, that image will live on in my brain, the way that even from behind you can see the love between them, the comfort each other's existence offers.

When we deliver the burgers, my father eats with gusto. Not so Frank, to whom I offer a burger a few times over. Each time, he waves it away with hands malformed by arthritis. But then I try breaking the burger up into pieces, and he eats it immediately. Ditto the onion chips. "Want another burger?" I ask Frank. They're awfully small—famously small—not for nothing is the advertising slogan "Eat 'em by the bagful!" But, "Oh, no," Frank says, holding his hand up, as though he's just polished off a gigantic platter heaped high with food.

As we drive Frank back to the nursing home, I listen as my sister talks to the driver. She thanks him for coming in on a Saturday, his day off, in order to drive the van, and she thanks him, too, for going above and beyond in getting Frank into the house in his wheelchair.

"No problem," he says. "They're interesting, those two. I hope when I get old, someone will come and take me out on my birthday."

Vicki gives him a nice tip, and says she'll send the realtor a picture she took of Frank and my dad, in the kitchen, smiling.

After we get my dad home, he falls asleep in his chair almost immediately. But we must awaken him soon afterward to go over to

Vicki's, where her husband, Derk, is making smoked ribs and pork chops; where there will be all kinds of side dishes, including my sister's famous potato salad and my niece's famous Greek salad, and where we intend to put ninety candles on the carrot cake I baked my dad. "I'm going to need help with that," I tell Bill. "Everyone will get a quadrant to light, and then we'll have my dad quick blow the candles out before the fire alarm goes off."

During the party, my mother sits behind a TV tray and does not say much of anything to anyone. I ask her if she'd like this or that to eat, and she refuses most of it.

When it's time for cake, four of us light the candles, and even before we are finished, the frosting starts melting. The candles are quickly melting down, too; there is wax all over the cake; you can feel the heat on your face. Never mind: we carry the blazing confection in and my father does a pretty good job blowing out the candles. We all applaud, and I think it's a pretty safe bet to say that at least a few of us are asking ourselves, **Do I want to live to be ninety?** I give my father a huge piece of cake, and he eats every bite.

In the car on the way home, my mother is chatting with me when my phone rings. It's my sister, saying, "Is she talking to you?"

I press my phone tighter to my ear. "Yeah. Uh-huh."

"Okay, so it's just me she's mad at," Vicki says.

"Why?"

"I have no idea. But she didn't say a word to me. Usually at these things she comes out in the kitchen to help, she talks to the little kids. But no. She wouldn't eat. She sat there scowling. She's probably pissed that he's getting all the attention."

But it's more than that, I think we both feel. It's that, lately, every day, she finds a way to be negative. And here's something else I think we both feel: Can't it just be my dad's day? It's his ninetieth birthday. Can't it just be **his day**?

The next morning, I get a call from Vicki. She won't say so, but I think she's been crying. She says, "I called Mom to see if you were there, and she was just . . . I said, 'What is your **problem**?' and she started in again with 'You people just leave me alone!' "

"We **should** leave her alone," I say bitterly.

"I'm afraid she'll take it out on Dad," Vicki says, and I fear that, too.

"I'll go over there and talk to her," I say.

"I'll come, too."

"Don't bother," I say. "Have a day for yourself."

"No," she says, "I'm coming, too."

On the way to the car, I pick some peonies from my parents' yard, to give to my mother: **Here. Does THIS help?**

On the ride over with Bill, I feel myself getting angrier and angrier. My sister has done so much for my mother, for both my parents. Why must my mother make her life harder? Why must she take so much for granted and be so unappreciative?

When we arrive, I find my parents in the kitchen. My father has a plate of waffles before him, and he's just begun to eat. My mother looks startled, then her face becomes closed, sour-looking. I give her the peonies and she says not much. This is in direct opposition to the woman on the elevator who so admired them; I gave her a couple to put in a bud vase, and you'd think I'd given her the world.

"I think Vicki's coming over," I say, and my mother says, "I hope not." We exchange a few testy words, and my father sits there. Finally he says, "Well, excuse me, but I'm going to eat," and takes a bite of his waffle.

My mother disappears and then comes back with a list that she shoves into my face. "Here! Here's my list of what you people think of me!"

I read a list that says we (even my dad!) find her selfish, uncaring, wallowing in self-pity, etc. I read through it, muttering, "Yup, sounds about right." And then I come to the bottom, where she has written, "I may just end it all if I can find a way."

I wish I could say that at that point my heart opens and I remind myself of all that she is having to endure. But all that happens is that I become infuriated. I feel as though everything we've tried to do for our mother is being ignored. Vicki calls just then, saying she is there, and I go downstairs to meet her in the lobby, my mother's list in hand.

"I brought her some chairs she wanted,"

Vicki says. "Is she in an awful mood? Because if she is, I'm not going up there."

"She's being horrible," I say. "But I want to show you something."

We sit in the chairs Vicki brought, and I show her the list. "Well," Vicki says. And then, again, "Well." And I can tell that she, too, is angry.

We take the elevator up, and then walk down the hall, fuming. We find Bill sitting with my father in the kitchen, and I give him a look that says, **Keep him there.** Vicki and I go into the television room, where we find our mother in her own furious state. "I don't want to talk to you," she says. And I say, "Well, you're going to."

And then I fling her list on a table and tell her that it is totally manipulative. That her behavior yesterday made Vicki feel terrible when Vicki had nothing to feel terrible about. My mother puts her fingers in her ears and, enraged, I pull her arm down and say, "No! You don't get to do that! You listen!"

Next comes a tirade from me and my sister that I am sure neither of us is proud of, but which, at the moment, anyway, we feel is overdue. We focus on our mother's constant complaining and criticizing, on her being unwilling to try the smallest things, of her being cruel to my dad. Which she emphatically denies. Which makes us even angrier.

"You purposely don't talk loud enough for him to hear," my sister says. "You walk ahead of him all the time. You know he has trouble walking and you won't slow down. It's like, **La-di-da, look how fast** I **can walk**. You say he shuffles like an old man. He can't help it!"

"You ignore him when he speaks to you," I say. "You pretend you don't hear him, when it's clear that you do. When he kisses you, you scowl. You think he doesn't see that? He knows you're angry at him all the time, and he doesn't know why!"

My mother says, "Shhhhhh!" and angrily points to the wall: **The neighbors!**

"I don't care!" I say, louder.

My mother lowers her voice and, in an attempt at reason, says, "As I have said before, I just wish you two could live here for a week and see what it's like."

Here my sister explodes. "I wish **you** could live **my** life for a week! I wish **you** could get up at six every morning to go to work, work overtime almost every night and then every weekend come here! And suicide? You think you're the only one who thinks of suicide? **Everyone** thinks of suicide at some point or another! But you know why people don't do it? Because it's selfish!"

"I **know** that!" my mother says. "That's why I haven't done it!"

I think about taking my mother up on her offer and living here for a week with my dad. I think, **I'd take him to bingo, and to breakfast and to dinner. I'd take him to watch Wii golf and to the men's group and to meet with the people who get together and talk every evening after dinner. I'd go for a walk with him and he could ride his scooter beside me.**

But I know there's more to it than that. I know there's a dark and dispiriting side of my father that she has to deal with all the time. She's eighty-eight years old and not even five feet tall. She just lost her sister and best friend and her house and she's losing her husband, bit by bit. She's under terrific strain, and it's manifesting in this anger: all that frustration and fear and sorrow has to go somewhere. But. She has also always been self-centered and pampered by my father, and now that some of my sister's and my fury has been unleashed, we can't seem to stop. It goes on and on, our accusations and recriminations.

Vicki says, "You say about Dad that he '**was** so intelligent.' He is **still** intelligent and this"—here her voice breaks—"this is **horrible** to watch. You just want him out of the way! You want him put into a nursing home so you don't have to take care of him!"

At this, my mother looks genuinely shocked. "No I don't!" she says. "I feel **sorry** for him! I suppose it's terrible to say this, but I just wish he'd go to sleep and not wake up!" Here she begins to weep loudly, and bows her head nearly to her lap.

It grows quiet. Finally, I say, "That's not horrible. That's how I wish he'd die, too. But in the meantime, we have to deal with what's going on."

My sister and I tell her what we are trying to do, what we hope to achieve, what we wish my mother would do to help on her end. And finally my mother raises her chin and speaks quietly. "Fine," she says. "I will try. I will try to do what you say."

There is no victory here. I think all three of us feel washed up on the shore, saved from drowning but, oh, scraped.

We go back into the kitchen. We've been ensconced in the TV room for a good half hour, forty minutes, and Bill now makes a much-needed trip to the bathroom—he was afraid to leave, lest my dad wander into our catfight. On our way back to Chicago, he tells me that my dad and he had a very nice conversation, and my dad was entirely lucid the whole time: no repetitions, no inappropriate remarks. Just a nice conversation.

I tell him about the not-so-nice conversation my sister, mother, and I had, and then I stare out the window, full of guilt. It's a long drive home.

What is your idea of God? When I was a child, I saw Him, as many do, as a benevolent grandfather: white beard, belted white robe, eyes that see everything, hands that can gentle any wild, cruel thing. **Would that God were that way,** I thought, driving down the freeway past the rest stops and gas stations, past the mile markers counting down the distance home. **Would that God would lay**

His hand on me and say, "I forgive you." Because I'm not sure I'll ever forgive myself. I see myself over and over knocking my mother's hand down from her plugging her ears, I see that familiar pattern of freckles on her white skin, her watch now loose about her wrist, I see the way that it was two against one, the way I wouldn't stop yelling, the way I'd lost my ability to be at all objective or empathetic. I thought about how, when the fight was over, she'd have no one to tell about it, because the people she enjoyed that kind of closeness with, had that kind of trust with, are all dead.

Yet sometimes such an awful fight is what it takes to clear the air. To defuse the situation. Or to blow it up so that you can put things back together again in a different way. Sometimes things get dire, and there are no easy solutions. I've heard about Hopi Indians who pray for rain by having priests run from a high mesa to the plains while grasping a handful of snakes. Sometimes, it seems, it works.

I call my mother from home the next day, and she is subdued. "I'm sending him downstairs to mail a letter now," she says. I hear her tell my dad, "The slot over by the letter boxes. If you don't see it, ask somebody, they'll help you." And then, "Maybe you'll run into someone to talk to!"

We both laugh a little, my mother and I, and the sound loosens the belt a notch.

She tells me that she's making some changes. She says she waited on my father all her life and that it would be good for him to do some things for himself.

"Right!" I say. It's true that she waited on him. She did the grocery shopping and made him all his meals, and for years delivered them to him either at the table or, later, to the TV tray as he sat watching television. If his beverage ran low, she refilled it. She performed all the tasks of the housewives of that era, like laundry, which meant washing and then hanging clothes and linens out on the line, even if they were frozen when you brought them in. She did the ironing (including sheets and my father's boxers and T-shirts). There was not much wash-and-wear then, nor were there steam irons, so you used a soda bottle with a sprinkler top for dampening the clothes, and if you weren't going to get to the huge pile of ironing in one day, you stored damp clothes in a plastic bag in the refrigerator. Women in those days vacuumed and dusted and scoured the sink and toilet daily. They cleaned the windows and washed and waxed the floors. Regarding the woman who comes in every other week to clean her apartment now, my mother says disdainfully, "Well, she uses a **mop** on the floors." Meaning she doesn't get on her hands and knees, as my mother did. The cleaning woman also doesn't burn her lungs using ammonia to clean out the oven, as my mother used to do—also on her hands and knees. Doesn't defrost the refrigerator or pull it out from the wall to dust its coils.

In her day, my mother performed an extra service, too. Growing up in my house, I often heard my father yelling, "Jeanne! Where'd I put my cigarette?!" He was a heavy smoker for many years, one of those guys who lit up immediately upon awakening: he'd sit at the side of the bed to have the first one of the day. Then he'd wander around getting ready for work, smoking the whole time, and oftentimes he'd forget where he'd put his cigarette down, so he'd yell for my mother. His tone was angry, accusatory: it was like it was her fault that he left his Camel on the edge of the dresser, or sink, or in some other completely nonsensical place. And when he yelled "Jeanne!" like that, she would scurry about trying to find his cigarette for him. Most times, she did. I wonder if he ever said, "Thanks, honey," or, "Sorry I yelled at you that way; I just got scared I'd set something on fire." I don't think so. I think he thought her finding his misplaced cigarettes was his due. So, yes, it might be nice for my father, even at this late date, to learn to help himself more.

My mother says, "Last night, he wanted one of those little ice-cream sundaes, you know those little turtle ice-cream sundaes I got at the grocery store? Well, he said he wanted one and I said, 'Go and get one.'"

"Good!" I say. "And while he's at it, he can get one for you."

Silence, while my mother mulls that over. What a notion! And then she says, "He's back." I hear her ask my father if ran into anyone to talk to. No.

JUNE 21, 2011

My father has an appointment tomorrow at the adult daycare center to see if they will accept him—and he them. I want to be there, it's an important day, and so once again I go to Minnesota, only this time I fly. My sister picks me up at the airport and we go out to dinner, where the talk focuses, as usual, on my parents. It reminds me of how my husband and I used to go out to get a break from our little children and then spend the entire time talking about our little children.

Vicki brings me to the assisted living place to spend the night on my parents' sofa. On the way in, we find a group of people sitting on the benches that flank the wide sidewalk leading into the building. They're enjoying the mild air, chatting, seemingly enjoying one another's company. It seems like such a pleasant thing, sitting out on a summer's eve, chatting with your neighbors. I wish my parents would join them once in a while. But they are ensconced in their apartment, as they are every night. Sitting there with the television blaring, oblivious to anything outside: neighbors talking, the sunset coloring the sky, the birds offering their final songs for the day.

"There are a lot of people sitting outside, talking!" Vicki says. **Would you like to join them?** I imagine she's thinking, and that's what I'm thinking, too. But my mother only mutters, "Well, good for them."

Oh, boy, here we go, I think. But then I recall a conversation I had with my daughter. She had spoken with my mother and then called me to say, "May I offer just one word of criticism? You have to stop pushing her! She'll do things when she's ready!" And when I heard Julie say that, I realized how often I **have** pushed my mother: calling her to remind her what's on the schedule that day, urging her to participate in activities in which she has no interest, to make friends with people I pick out for her. So now, when Vicki speaks so enthusiastically of the people sitting outside, I hear it as my mother might: another directive, offered by someone who doesn't have a clue. I make a vow not to suggest anything for her to do while I'm here.

Before I go to bed, I have a long talk with my mother and try very hard to just listen. She loosens up gradually, and whereas she begins by complaining, she ends by telling me some of the good things she's been doing, and about the two women she talks to almost daily. Peace.

JUNE 22, 2011

"It's very nice to meet you, Art," the social worker at the adult daycare center says, shaking my father's hand. We're in her office, after having been greeted at the door of the daycare center by the man called "the official greeter." He's a bit overly enthusiastic and wild-eyed, but hey.

It was a little sad at first, walking in: there were men there who were gorked out, there were men who were physically quite incapacitated. I had not wanted my father to be the worst one there, to be fumbling with his memory among a group of men who had no such difficulty. Now I worry that he'll be the best one there. It's an uncharitable feeling, I suppose. Mostly, what I'm hoping is that my father will find a friend. I feel like my daughter, who has worries about her children integrating into nursery school.

In the office, we talk about what my father might expect, coming here, and see the schedule, which has some activities daily: current events, exercise, lunch. Other things change daily: musicians come, there are Wii sports. We talk about what the center expects from my dad in return, which isn't much, really: just show up as often as you can and try to participate. We talk about transportation and fill out forms and decide that we will go over to the Metro Mobility offices to turn in the form today, to see if we can expedite the service. Then, for six dollars a day, a bus will pick my father up and bring him home, too.

My father is friendly and agreeable; he says he'll try it. I think three of us—my mom, my sister, and I—all heave a sigh of relief. Maybe four, counting the social worker.

After dropping off the Metro Mobility forms, we have lunch at a Mexican restaurant. My mother points to a table over by the wall and says, "That's where we sat." I know what she means. **Before.** Back when they could go out by themselves whenever they felt like it, back when they weren't so dependent on everyone else, back when they could both read the menus and confusion of any sort was not an issue.

After lunch, we head over to my parents' house. There are some things my mother wants to salvage from the imminent estate sale, and we figure we'll set those things aside in an empty bedroom and keep the door closed when the masses come to fight over what my parents will have to part with.

The realtor has given my mother the name of an auctioneer, and I call and ask if he can meet with us. It turns out he's free at five p.m., so we decide to do some work sorting things for a couple of hours. After that I'll take my parents home to their apartment, and then come back to the house so Vicki and I can meet with the guy.

On the way up the steps to the backyard, I am behind my father and it's a good thing I am—he starts to tip backward, and were I not there, he would have fallen. Hard. I think, **We got them out in the nick of time.** As my father slowly climbs the second set of steps into the house, he pauses on the middle step and looks around at the yard, then into the little sun porch off the kitchen. "It's a nice house," he says. "If I were looking, I'd probably buy it again."

There is a way that someone looks at a thing he has owned and loved, something that he took care of and cherished, that is no longer his. That's how my father looks at the yard where he fed so many birds and finally surrendered to the squirrels, feeding them, too. That's how he regards the sun porch, where he sat listening to baseball games on the radio, and eating summer dinners: barbeque chicken and corn on the cob, fat slices of tomatoes that he grew himself. Pesto made from the basil he also grew. That look he gives the house is sweeping and slow, full of gratitude and sorrow. I don't think I ever really saw that look before, the way I see it now. See it and feel it myself, in my own small way.

My dad steps into the kitchen and, arms trembling, lowers himself into the booth. He knows he's not capable of helping us up in the attic, so he sits and stares patiently ahead, and waits. I think memory movies must be running in his head, and I leave him to his private ruminations.

I check on him a couple of times, and one time when I come down, he's gone. I find him in the front yard, his hands on his hips, inspecting a face he made years ago on a tall tree: plastic eyes, a nose and a mouth. I think he might have put it there for the entertainment of the neighborhood kids, or maybe as a gently ironic lawn decoration. Now he stands looking at it as though he's expecting he might have a conversation with Mr. Tree.

"Dad," I say, gently.

He turns around and looks at me.

"Want to come back in?"

He climbs the stairs slowly. I don't trust that he won't fall again (I'm so grateful he didn't fall before), and I hold on to his elbow. At first, he resists my doing this. Then he pretends not to notice it, and so do I.

"Could you help a little with the sorting?" I ask.

"Sure," he says.

"Mom needs to know what hats you'd like to keep, if any," I say, and hand him a pile of hats. He tries one on, a straw hat with a colorful fabric band.

"That looks good," I say.

He nods. "Panama." Then he tries on the

next hat, and the one after that. He puts every one of them in the **keep** pile. Every single one.

I need to find a computer so that I can do a little work, and I take my dad with me to the library. "Ever been here before?" I ask him, as we pull up to the building. "Nope," he says, looking it over.

"Nice, isn't it?" I say, and he says, "Um-hum."

I find him a nice-looking chair by the window where I can see him from the computer. "Want a book to look at?" I ask, and he says no, he'll just wait. I find him a book anyway, one on fantastical tree houses that people have built, and he sits looking at the pictures with real interest. He's so engaged, in fact, that I hate to make him stop looking when it's time to go. "Want to check that book out?" I ask him, and he says, "No. No." For a moment, I consider doing it anyway, but don't.

We go back to the house to collect my mother, and then I drive them both back to their apartment. My mother has descended into crabbiness again. Must have been hard to be in the house and know she's not going back. **Maybe she'll just be this way now**, I think. **I give up.**

When I get back to the house after having dropped my parents off, the auctioneer arrives promptly. There are some people who are doing their show from the moment you meet them, and this man is one of them. He's smarmy and glib and he says my sister's and my names like he now has ownership of a good percentage of our personas. He goes through the house quickly; it's clear he's not impressed with the little pilgrims my mother used to put on the table at Thanksgiving. He flips through my dad's remaining stamp albums, and says, "American. Where are the European?" Or maybe it's the other way around. But whichever way, it's clear that my dad has sold all the good ones; these are just not worth much. "Sorry to say," the guy says, "but you can get just about anything online now. It decreases the value. You know?"

"Oh, uh-huh," I say.

He looks at my dad's watchmaker's bench and this interests him quite a bit, until we tell him my brother wants that. Then he opens and shuts the drawers at great speed, saying, "Where are the watches?" He looks down his nose at the watch parts, saying, "These might have **some** value."

"How about the clocks?" we ask, referring to my dad's beloved collection of them. "Maybe the grandfather one," the auctioneer says.

He digs around in another room of the basement, and my heart is just aching at the speed at which he reviews my parents' lifelong possessions, at the way he dismisses my mother's Lovelace crystal glasses, which she got for her hope chest at eighteen. "I wouldn't bother," he says. "The whole collection is worth maybe seventy-five dollars." He holds one glass up and sees a small chip and frowns. "That'll take your **lip** off," he says. **Unless you have the vast intelligence to drink from another one of the glasses,** I want to say. **Unless you can forgive a slight imperfection for the glory of the history of the thing.** I think about my friend Marianne, who was asked by an old lady if she would like to take the woman's fabric— she couldn't see to sew anymore. Marianne said, "So I allowed four hours and I—"

"Four hours!" I said. "Why would it take you four hours to pick it up?"

Marianne shrugged. "I knew she'd want to tell me about each piece of fabric. You know: 'This is what I made my daughter's prom dress out of. This is what I used for curtains in the sun parlor.'"

Whatever Marianne is, this man is the polar opposite. I don't expect him to linger, rhapsodizing over each item. I don't even mind his speed. But if he could just acknowledge that there is more here than fabric and glass, metal and wood. There's a personal history, memories of a time that will never return, a time that meant so much to so many. These things he's rifling through make up my parents' little empire, and the flag is still flying. But I guess my sister is okay with the guy: she has been quietly following him around, voicing no objection, so I figure we'll have to work with him—I feel it's my sister's right to call the shots, as she's the one who lives here and deals most often with my parents. But then he bends over to sneer at something else, and Vicki, who is standing behind him where he can't see her, looks impassively over at me while she flips the guy off.

After his whirlwind tour, after he has

finished deriding my mother's collector plates and garden fountain and my father's piles of **National Geographic**s and his massive collection of golf balls and hats, he says, "Tell you what. I'll take the stamp collection, the spinning wheel, the clocks, the watch parts, the snow blower, the German beer mugs, the crockery, the lawn furniture, the wooden folk art figures, and the wicker porch set. Five hundred dollars."

"Yeah. We'll call you if we're interested," I say, escorting him as quickly as I can to the door.

After he walks out, I look over at my sister. "Asshole," I say.

"Agreed," she says.

That night, I am on the couch and my parents think I'm asleep in preparation for a very early flight, but I'm not. I hear my father say, "Aren't I supposed to take some pills?" He's referring to the meds he's meant to take at bedtime.

My mother is in her recliner, watching

baseball. "It's too late now," she says. A pause, and then my father says, "Well, I'm going to take my pills."

I go in and confront my mother. "You weren't going to give him his pills?"

She is surprised, caught. She mumbles some excuse, and I say, "I'll help him," and I do. Then I lie on the couch and worry about how many other times this has happened, or will.

I go to sleep but then wake up at three-thirty and can't fall back asleep. At five, I tiptoe out of the apartment and head downstairs to meet the cab I ordered last night. I feel happy, optimistic, and this surprises me. Usually, when I'm short on sleep, my mood is not good. The cabdriver and I have an interesting conversation; he tells me he's from Uganda and that he starts work at three a.m. and sometimes waits two or three hours for his first fare. Despite the difficulties of the job he's doing, he couldn't be more pleasant; he seems to be one of those people who are just happy to be alive on the spinning planet. The sky pinkens, then turns pale blue, and as I get out of the cab and head into the termi-nal, I turn my thoughts from Minnesota and my parents to my life in Chicago. Bill. My dogs. My work. My house and my garden and my friends.

On the plane, I don't sleep, which also surprises me. I never have trouble sleeping on planes. I look out the window at the cloud art and ponder why I am so curiously well rested. I decide it's because I slept under the same roof as my parents. Compromised as they may be now, I nevertheless slid into that child's privileged way of thinking that my mother and my father were there in the nighttime, watching over me.

JULY 18, 2011

Last week when I called my mother, she told me about how she had prepared a lunch platter for her former next-door neighbors, who came over to show her their new baby. She was still in low-gear party mode, listlessly describing the kind of lunchmeat she had offered, but describing it nonetheless. When I asked her about the little baby, my mother said, "Well, he's not a pretty baby, but he's a smiley baby." She reminded me in that instant of my grandmother, her mother, who, upon seeing my firstborn, said, "That's the ugliest baby I ever saw."

The neighbors who visited said an interesting thing to my mother. Apparently in reaction to her saying she didn't much like it there, they said, "Oh, we would have taken care of you." As innocently as they may have offered that remark, as good-heartedly, it did a great deal of damage.

First of all, it made my mother start thinking again that living in that house was possible. It made her believe it would be simple, now that someone had signed up for duty. It put my mother right back on the hamster wheel of being unable to commit to being where she was, of thinking and thinking about how she might move back.

"Mom," I said. "Do you really think they could take care of you?"

"Yes!" she said.

And for once, I didn't get into it. I didn't say one thing about a woman with a new baby hardly having time to go to the bathroom. I didn't mention the fact that they have other children to attend to, that they go on vacations, that they would not be thrilled to be called in the middle of the night, that they are not home all the time, and that you can't schedule emergencies. Nor did I point out that my mother hadn't even known her neighbor was pregnant, so how close could they be? "Okay," I said.

It was a beautiful day there, I happened to know, and I asked my mother if she had been outside at all. "Nothing to see but cars," she said.

"Out back?" I said. "In the garden?"

"Oh, I don't know," she said bitterly.

I mentioned that things might get easier when my dad starts going to the adult day-care center twice a week.

"Well, I'm just waiting for the state government to shut down. Then there'll be no transportation, so that will be that," she said. It was true that there had been talk of that.

Silence. I closed my eyes and rubbed my forehead. Then my mother told me she'd been to a residents' meeting.

"Really," I said. "How was it?"

"They talked about how they didn't like that the people who served them in the dining room had tattoos," my mother said. "So they're going to make them wear long sleeves. And they complained that there wasn't enough egg in the potato salad. I wanted to say, 'Hey, people, get a life!'"

I had to agree with her there, although potato salad without enough egg is a serious offense in my book, too.

That evening, I sat on a bench that I keep in the back part of my yard, next to a bank of hydrangeas, many of which finally came in blue this year. Others are lavender, or dusty pink, or hot pink, or a near red. They are so beautiful, it almost hurts to look at them. I kept moving my eyes over the hydrangeas: here, there, everywhere, as one does when looking at an art quilt.

I was waiting for the fireflies to come out and the very back of the garden seemed like a good place to sit—from there, I had a full view of where they like to go, in and out of the blossoms. It was still light enough that the first firefly had yet to appear, and when I could finally tear my eyes away from the hydrangeas, I stared at the back of my house, which was awash in a kind of pinkish light. I thought about each room inside the house, and then I admired the construction of the outside. It's an American foursquare, my house, which I think of as architecture's declarative sentence. I thought about how I would feel if I were told I could no longer manage living in my house and would have to move. Some part of me leaped up to say, "I **would** move! I'm sick of all these possessions, all these stairs! I want to simplify my life!" Another part of me knew the sorrow it would bring, and I think part of the sorrow is that when you are told you have to leave your house, you are being told you have to leave a part of yourself. Mostly, though, I thought about how the idea of having to leave my house feels about as real to me as getting old does to a fourteen-year-old.

I sat quietly for a long time with my hands in my lap, staring at my house. And then the fireflies came out and I switched my attention to those magical bits of moving light, landing here, landing there, occasionally shooting up like elegant little flares, but never staying anywhere too long, lest they be captured and taken to somewhere they'd rather not be.

The state government does indeed close down, but Metro Mobility services remain. On my father's first day of riding the bus to adult daycare (which, in the interest of dignity and machismo, we call "the VA center") my mother reports that she gets him up early so that he has plenty of time to get ready. She makes him a breakfast of oatmeal and cinnamon toast. She tucks the money he needs for the ride out in one pocket, and the money he needs for the ride home in another. She writes his address and phone number on a piece of paper, which she puts in yet another pocket. She goes downstairs with him fifteen minutes early to wait for the bus. She sees that he is helped onto the bus and safely seated, and then she goes back upstairs to the apartment to call the center to make sure someone will watch for him and escort him in. Then she goes to the house to meet with another auctioneer, and this one she likes. He's kind, he takes his time, and best of all, he makes sure she understands that her job in all this is to do nothing: he will set things up, sell them, and dispose of the things that don't sell.

When my father returns from daycare, he is happy: he won two dollars at bingo. He liked the current events program. He liked the place.

The next time, he was not quite as enthusiastic about it; then, on the day before what was to be the third visit, he told my mother he didn't think he'll go. "Oh, yes you will," she said, and he did. On that day, he fell asleep during the current events part, and he didn't get to play Wheel of Fortune, because time ran out. But he had gone and he seemed to have accepted the fact that he would continue to go, in large part because he knew it would help my mother. He had fought in World War II, he had been in Korea, and now he had to do his hardest tour of duty yet. Last time I talked to him about how it went at the center, he said, "Pretty good!" and I was so happy. "Did they have some dancers there this time?" I asked, and he said, "Yeah, and they were good. It was five women and one man."

"I'll bet **that** guy's happy!" I said, and my dad chuckled and said, "Guess so!" And then he said, "How are **you** doing?" and I told him and he listened carefully, because he is still my dad and he is still taking care of me.

A few days later, I have a conversation with my mother about her and my dad moving to a condo when their house sells. "We don't want you to be miserable," I say. "And if you're not going to take advantage of any of the things offered here, why pay for them? We can move you to a ground-floor condo, where there's a screened-in porch where you can have your container garden. Metro Mobility can come there to pick Dad up."

My mother says no, she will stay where she is. She also says would like to try embroidery, and so I send her some skeins of floss and some needles and a hoop. I also send her some yarn and knitting needles, in case she would like to join the group of women who knit sweaters for charity every Friday.

She has made a new friend named Betty who still drives, which is the high school equivalent of being head cheerleader and prom queen and president of the student body and highest-ranking member of the National Honor Society. My mother has also signed up to go to Byerly's grocery store on the bus, and sometimes she sits at the kitchen table to play double solitaire with my dad. When I hear all this, Cat Stevens comes into my head: **Morning has broken like the first morning.**

I get a phone call from my friend Marianne this morning. Much of our conversation focuses, as it always does, on our parents and on our children. Marianne's father died many years ago, and her mother, Fina, a fiery, hyperenergetic Italian, began to lose her marbles a few years ago.

Here is an example of the old Fina. Once when I was out in California, Marianne and I drove to Santa Rosa to visit her. When Marianne called to tell her we were coming, she said, "Now, don't **cook**, Ma. We're both on diets and we only want salad. Just make a **salad**."

"Okay," Fina said, and she did make a salad, as promised. She also made homemade focaccia, pizza, lasagna, a couple of pies, and biscotti. The woman lived alone and had a huge kitchen, and every cupboard was full to the bursting point. And if you went out to the garage, which was a big two-car garage, you'd find more cupboards all along the wall, also jammed full. She used to go for her swim early in the morning, then come home and make pizza and bring it over to the bocce court. She had theme parties at the drop of the hat, and the cuisine always matched the theme.

But then she began getting confused about how to take her pills and, soon, about lots of other things. It became dangerous. Marianne finally got her into an independent living place near her. It was murder getting her there; Fina didn't want to leave her house, didn't see why she couldn't still climb her fig tree in order to trim the branches, or cook vats of red sauce, or drive all over tarnation. She is in Nebraska now, visiting her sisters, and Marianne is worried that they can't take care of her. She says Fina is in constant motion, rummaging in her purse, cleaning the sink, wandering off to do this, or do that, and the aunts are compromised in their own ways. But she'll be back in California in a couple of days, and then Marianne will be in charge of taking care of her again, which is a blessing and a burden.

Marianne says that when she goes over to her mom's place to take her somewhere, Fina does her bee dance. "You know how bees do that dance?" Marianne says. "That's what my mom is like. I'm trying to get her **out the door** and she says, 'Wait, I gotta wee. Wait, I need my Kleenex. Wait, I need my cough drops. Where are my keys?'" And sometimes Marianne gets really impatient, as anyone would. You want to be like Ignatius of Loyola, who said, "Teach us to give and not to count the cost," but you end up more often like Bette Davis in **What Ever Happened to Baby Jane?** Recently, on a day when Marianne was trying to hustle her mother up, Fina began to cry—and this is a woman who **never** cries. "What's wrong, Ma?" Marianne asked, and Fina said, "I don't make you happy."

"It broke my heart," Marianne says. "She's still so buoyant and positive and can-do. She's actually fun to be around, unless you have anything else to do."

She tells me about an eighty-five-year-old woman she knows who is getting a divorce from her ninety-six-year-old husband. She can't take care of him anymore, and he won't cooperate with anything she suggests. "She just wants to sit and read," Marianne says. "She just wants some peace in her life."

I think, **That's what my mother wants, too.**

After a few more minutes of talking about how hard it is to manage oldsters, how draining it is to be the sandwich generation, I've suddenly had enough.

"What did you have for breakfast?" I ask Marianne.

"Blueberries and coffee," she says.

"That's it?" I ask.

"Yeah," she says.

"Well, I'm going downstairs to make me some pancakes," I say. And that's what I do.

A phone call to my parents. I talk first to my father, who tells me about the doctors' appointments both of them had, and about how the extremely hot weather there is moderated by the presence of so many trees around them. "The halls are warm, but the apartment is comfortable." He tells me my mother has gone down for the mail, but she comes back as we're talking, and he gives her the phone.

She tells me that the eye doctor wasn't too optimistic about either of them, but she went to the on-site library and found a couple of large-print books. She tells me my father went to the ice-cream social without her, as she was somewhere else, and that they both went to the watermelon social. "I was the only one to put salt on mine," she says, laughing. She tells me that on Friday she will wait for the bus that will take my father to the VA center, and that then she will take the bus to Byerly's supermarket. "I like Byerly's," she says. "They have the meatloaf mix that has the lamb in it. And they have veal roast, so I'm going to get some and make wiener schnitzel. And they are the only store that has spaetzle, so I'll make that, too."

"A German feast!" I say. "You should make apfelkuchen, too."

"You know," she says, "there's a ninety-seven-year-old woman living here who's from Germany, and she does all her own cooking from scratch. And her specialty is apfelkuchen!"

"Where's **she** live?" I ask, and my mother says, "On five," with a measure of . . . what? Pride? (**Look where I live!**) Comfort? (**I can just go right up and ask for the recipe.**) Contentment? (**Don't worry. Turns out I have all I need here.**)

My mother says that for dinner tonight, she's going to have some ham and dumpling soup that her grandson's wife, Mandy, made, and some chocolate cake that she also made. And that tonight, since the Twins aren't playing, she'll give that embroidery a try.

I know, as anyone reading this knows, that at some point things will get worse for my parents. My father may need to move to an Alzheimer's unit. My mother might. Either one of them could sicken or die at any moment. But whatever your age, you are picnicking with your back to a forest full of bears, and right now, I think my parents are as good as they can possibly be. My father is here, fairly alert and oriented. My mother is back to herself, grateful for the taste of watermelon on a sweltering summer day, deeply involved in baseball, talking about books, looking forward to starting a new hobby. She and my father seem easy with each other. I think they have gotten to the place of peace I wanted so much for both of them to find—and they have found it not apart from but with each other. I think they have moved back into a love they have shared for almost seventy years. And I think they have come to understand that when the sweet moments come now, they are sweeter than ever they were before, because there is not a chance in the world that they will be taken for granted.

They are resigned to the fact that the house will be sold, and when it is, I intend to go over and visit the new owners with beautiful gifts. One of those gifts, I hope, will be that my parents will come with me, and they will welcome the new people and share information about the best places to go in the neighborhood and in this way give them their blessing. I think it was Robert Frost who said that everything he had learned about life could be summed up in three words: it goes on.

I have a friend whose elderly mother lives with her and is driving her crazy. Her mother was once a talented artist, an intellectual with myriad interests. Now, my friend says, "she gets up in the morning and makes a cup of coffee and she's so slow, doing it. I mean, I just watch her sometimes to see how she can possibly be so **slow**. Then she sits at the kitchen table and talks about what might be for lunch. I just can't stand it! All she talks about is her cup of coffee in the morning and the weather and what her next meal will be. I really wonder . . . is there any meaning to the end of life?"

I suppose one way to answer that question is to think about how a baby's meaning in life is a ray of sunshine, the color red, the nearness of his mother's flesh. For a teenager, it is music, fitting in, hormone management. In midlife, meaning comes from focusing on our families, our jobs, our involvement with the world outside our kitchens. Which is to say that the meaning of life is ever-changing, even as we are. Who's to say that the richest time of life might not be when a cup of morning coffee fills the world? If you found a holy man hidden away on a mountain who found fulfillment in such seemingly simple things, would you not admire him?

It is a very warm summer morning, and my parents are both alive and ambulatory. They are still capable of enjoying a slice of apple pie and of having a conversation. They are living together in what will probably be the last home they will ever share. Imagine them at the kitchen table. My mother will serve breakfast on the embroidered tablecloth. The day will pass. Laundry will be done, the mail will be gotten, the phone will be answered; people they pass in the hall will be acknowledged. Lunch and dinner will be eaten. Someone may drop by for a visit. In the evening, the television will be on and they will sit watching their shows. They will go to bed together—my father has never and will not now go to bed without my mother—and while the moon follows an ancient path across the night sky, they will lie next to each other with their eyes closed. In the morning, the first thing they see will be each other.

Epilogue

My dad died in the early-morning hours on December 26, 2012, after having enjoyed, to the extent that he was able, a Christmas gathering at his and my mom's place. By then, he was using oxygen and a wheelchair or a walker. He slept in a hospital bed that had been set up in the TV room, and a caregiver came at night so that my mom could get some sleep. When he went to bed that night, after bidding farewell to his guests, he was joined for a while by his wife and her sister Lala, who sat on either side of him, each holding one of his hands. I came into the room at one point to see if they needed anything but then walked right out. It was too tender what was happening there; it was private.

On the night he died, the caregiver asked at one point if my dad was hungry. "I'm not," he said, "but you go ahead and eat." Then he made many suggestions as to what she might enjoy. Later, he asked the caregiver if she liked to fish, and he told her he had just had a lovely dream about fishing with his brother. Later still, he asked to go to the bathroom. The caregiver told him she would help him use the bedside commode, and my father said no, he wanted to go to the bathroom. He insisted upon it. Halfway there, using his walker, he turned to the caregiver, said, "I'm not going to make it," and slipped to the floor and died.

My mom died March 15, 2015, in hospice, at the same place where her sister Lala died. I had flown home for the weekend to get a bigger suitcase and my computer so that I could work while my mom was sleeping. We all thought it was fine, because she was doing so well at that point that we had entertained taking her out of hospice. But she died rather suddenly when I was gone. She complained of pain in her midsection, took in a big breath and was gone. In her room were many flowers, her beloved books on tape, and photos, including one of her and my father on their wedding day. How young and strong and beautiful they were, she in her yellow dress and her brown velvet hat, my father in his Army uniform, too fierce to smile. My brother and sister were with our mom when she died, and Frank Sinatra was crooning softly in the background. (My father was always very jealous of Frank Sinatra, because my mom loved him so.)

The last words I said to my mom were, "I'll miss you," and she said, "I'll miss you, too."

I do miss her. I find, in fact, that I miss both my parents far more than I thought I would. It's not in the acute way I did when they first died. Now it's more of feeling like I've had a glimpse of something about them that escaped me when they were alive.

It might be a memory of something that really happened. For example, after my father died and we were helping my mother clean some things out of the apartment, I came across a flyswatter bedecked with plastic daisies. "Do you want this?" I asked, holding it up.

"Yes," she said, and took it from me and lay it on the table with great care. "Your father made that for me in daycare." She stood looking at it for a moment, then went on with sorting. I stood looking at it, and a thousand things occurred to me about the way that even in bitterness and confusion and anger, my parents' love for each other endured. I saw that whenever I was looking at them, I was seeing only the tip of the iceberg. They belonged to each other more than they belonged to us. I had once asked my mother if she still had the letters my dad sent to her when he was in World War II, when he was in Korea. "No," she said. "They're gone." But I think what she meant was that she could see the drooling writer in me and those letters were none of my or anyone else's business. And she was right.

Other times, I imagined something that nonetheless felt true. Not long after my mom died, I was in St. Paul, Minnesota, for a literary event. I was staying in a hotel where I could walk to Mickey's Diner, a legendary place serving comfort food in a vintage train car twenty-four hours a day. I had always wanted to go, but never had. I ordered a platter that had pancakes, sausage, and eggs, and coffee. While I was listening with pleasure to the conversations around me, my father and mother moved to sit on the stools beside me, never mind that they were occupied by someone else; now they were doubly occupied. My father was in a nice short-sleeved sports shirt, orange sherbet in color. It was neatly pressed, as his shirts always were; I never saw that man dressed in anything that was not clean and pressed. The hankies he kept in his back pocket were spotless and folded just so. But there he was, his hands clasped loosely on the counter before him. My mother sat with her hands in her lap. "This is good," I told my parents, referring to my oversized breakfast platter. "Yeah, it always was a good place," my dad said. Then, looking at my mother, he said, "So?," only he said it "Zo?," making it sound a bit Deutsch. It was how he used to ask her if she was ready to go. My mother stood, and they disappeared.

When I started the walk back to my hotel room, my mother came back in diminutive form to ride on my shoulder for a while. "So much of what you love is everywhere around you," she said. "But, you know, I always meant to tell you, you need to loosen your laces and let yourself be loved back. And you need to understand that love isn't just one thing."

She was right. I am crippled in love relationships by fear, by defense, by doubt, by my own lack of self-regard. It makes me constantly want to abandon ship. I hope that in understanding more about my parents, even though—or perhaps because—they are gone, I'll learn lessons about faith and endurance and trust and forgiveness. About putting **I** aside for the sake of **we**. About how love circles back on itself over and over to create deeper definitions of itself. And I hope I'll learn the value of that hardest thing of all: seeing it through.

Acknowledgments

I want to thank Phyllis Florin for her enthusiastic support of this book. Thanks, too, to the many others who read the manuscript and said, "This would help so many people." I hope it does. Finally, I want to thank my parents for putting up with my efforts during a trying time, and for setting the example of how an extraordinary love works. I see them still.

ABOUT THE AUTHOR

ELIZABETH BERG is the author of many bestselling novels, including **The Confession Club, Night of Miracles, The Story of Arthur Truluv, Open House** (an Oprah's Book Club selection), **Talk Before Sleep,** and **The Year of Pleasures,** as well as the short story collection **The Day I Ate Whatever I Wanted**. **Durable Goods** and **Joy School** were selected as ALA Best Books of the Year. She adapted **The Pull of the Moon** into a play that enjoyed sold-out performances in Chicago and Indianapolis. Berg's work has been published in thirty-one countries, and three of her novels have been turned into television movies. She is the founder of Writing Matters, a quality reading series dedicated to serving author, audience, and community. She teaches one-day writing workshops and is a popular speaker at venues around the country. Some of her most popular Facebook postings have been collected in **Make Someone Happy, Still Happy,** and **Happy to Be Here**. She lives outside Chicago.

elizabeth-berg.net
Facebook.com/bergbooks

LIKE WHAT YOU'VE READ?

Try these titles by Elizabeth Berg,
also available in large print:

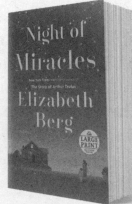

Night of Miracles
ISBN 978-0-525-63178-1

The Confession Club
ISBN 978-0-593-17099-1

**The Story of
Arthur Truluv**
ISBN 978-1-5247-8303

For more information on large print titles, visit
www.penguinrandomhouse.com/large-print-format-book